Zoo Careers

Zoo Careers

WILLIAM BRIDGES

CURATOR OF PUBLICATIONS EMERITUS
NEW YORK ZOOLOGICAL SOCIETY

William Morrow and Company | New York

Printed in the United States of America.
Library of Congress Catalog Card Number 71-155989
Design by Cynthia Basil

1 2 3 4 5 75 74 73 72 71

This book is dedicated to the memory of
Lee S. Crandall,
General Curator Emeritus of the New York
Zoological Park, and my friend;
and to the young people who may someday
follow in his footsteps.
They can have no more shining beacon.

Contents

Zoo Careers

Foreword

Over almost a third of a century I have received—and answered—a great many letters from young people wanting to know whether their interest in natural history might find an outlet through work in a zoological park. This book is an attempt to tell what the opportunities are, how to prepare for them, and what one typically does in a zoo.

Perhaps, here and there, I will appear to be "selling" the satisfactions of a zoo career a little too hard. I can only say that while presumably everybody who is doing work he enjoys thinks he has the best job in the world, zoo people are especially likely to have that feeling highly developed. And for one main reason: directly or indirectly, they have something to do with living wild animals, with their endless capacity to surprise, perplex, amuse, and instruct.

But make no mistake about it: there are headaches in the zoo business, as in any other. An animal man can never escape the responsibility he has for the lives and well-being of hundreds, perhaps thousands, of living creatures, and he must always anticipate the worst. Publications people have deadlines. Budget-making time always seems to be staring the business office in the face. Still, when pressures build up, it is at least theoretically possible to slip out and "look at the animals" for a few minutes and envy them their freedom from work and worry and inconsiderate bosses. Or zoo people may catch a whiff of lion or elephant on their way to the parking lot at quitting time and be reminded that, at any rate, it is better than breathing the gasoline fumes of a city street. Zoos are, after all, well named as "gardens" or "parks," and there are worse surroundings in which to spend one's working hours.

A job in a zoo has another small but not inconsiderable bonus: you automatically become an expert on all wild animal life and behavior, and at dinner parties you will be asked everything your fellow guests always wanted to know about animals. Of course, if you are in the nonanimal side of the zoo operation, you had better make sure no real animal expert is present before you become too pontifical.

You will live and work in the company of knowledgeable and in the main dedicated people. Some of them will have traveled to far and interesting parts of the world, either to study animals or to capture them. Such opportunities may come to you, too—in time. However, it might as well be said right here that being sent on a collecting trip to the tropics is not a routine expectation for anyone on a zoo staff. Only the largest zoos, in search of great and otherwise unobtainable rarities, are likely to have the money and the staff to equip a collecting expedition. Most animals come to a zoo as a result of quite unexciting telephone calls or letters between the zoo and professional collectors or animal dealers.

In a world of rabid and ferocious competition, the zoo man is in the happy position of giving, not trying to get. Giving recreation and information—and yes, even amusement—to people who increasingly need to get away from the competitive life and the sterility of steel and glass and concrete of the cities.

For a zoo should be looked upon as an outpost of the earth's basic life-support system protruding into the artificiality of a city. No city could survive a day on its own ecological resources; it has no intrinsic food production, water, power, oxygen. A zoo can, and must, make people aware of the realities of the environmental sciences. And it is today the only place where most city people will ever get any firsthand view of wildlife, or any idea of wild places.

The zoo man is dealing with the basic and natural world, and as he turns more and more to an active participation in conservation (as zoos are doing), he can feel that he is spending his life well and to a worthy purpose.

W. B.

Pleasantville, New York

1971

CHAPTER ONE

The Structure of a Zoo

There are more than 200 recognized zoological parks in the United States and they employ about 4000 persons as staff. Staff includes everyone from director to night watchman—all the permanent employees—and the people directly concerned with the animals are outnumbered by those in the ancillary services. Still, there are a lot of jobs for both "animal men" and "animal women," and a zoo career is an entirely practicable goal for anyone who prepares himself for it.

This book assumes that the animal side of the operation is the chief interest of anyone thinking of a zoo career. Nevertheless, some of the auxiliary jobs are discussed, for in one sense everyone who works in a zoo is concerned with the animals; they are the reason his job exists. A restaurant manager who overlooked a barrage of publicity about an important new animal acquisition might be embarrassed to find he had not laid in provisions for unusually large crowds of visitors. Or a zoo business manager might someday find himself appointed director. It has happened.

There is no standard table of organization for all zoos. Titles and responsibilities vary. However, for simplicity and with particular reference to the animal operations, the chain of command may be defined thus: director, who has overall responsibility; perhaps an assistant director who carries some of the administrative burdens; curators who head their respective departments of mammals, birds, and reptiles; possibly associate or assistant curators who carry part of the load; head keepers of mammals, birds, and reptiles; keepers who do the actual work of feeding and watering and cleaning. There may be a full-time veterinarian, or perhaps a local practitioner is engaged on a part-time basis or is called in when needed.

All these jobs require education and training. No one is likely to become a curator of mammals or birds or reptiles without formal education and practical experience in his subject. He can get "book learning" in high school and college, and sometimes training by starting at the bottom as a keeper and working his way to the top, even to the position of director. Of course, political appointments to posts in zoos are not unheard of—some have turned out to be excellent choices, too—but on the curator level it is a good deal better to have specialized training and actual experience. Otherwise something might bite you.

Because I have spent thirty-one years, the longest and most enjoyable part of my working life, as curator of publications in the New York Zoological Park (Bronx Zoo) and therefore know it best, I have chosen to go into most detail about the jobs in that zoo. It may not be typical (what *is* the "typical" zoo?) but its people do about the same things that staffs do in other zoos, plus some that are not usual in smaller institutions.

Apart from the conventional animal departments, the

Bronx Zoo has, for example, a large library and a professional librarian, Departments of Education and of Publications
and Public Relations, two full-time photographers, a photo
librarian, a membership chairman, a personnel manager, a
sizeable Department of Exhibition and Graphic Arts, and a
printshop equipped for both letterpress and offset printing.
Then there are the more general nonanimal services of construction and maintenance (metal workers, carpenters, plumbers, electricians, automobile mechanics and drivers, painters, gardeners, groundsmen, gate attendants, and night
watchmen), purchasing agent, restaurant manager, souvenir
supervisor, business office personnel, and secretaries, which
add up to quite a lot of zoo jobs. The Bronx Zoo does indeed have a permanent staff of about 250 persons, and this is
more than doubled for temporary summertime operation.

The animal side of the best modern zoos calls for the combined talents of a naturalist, an educator, and a conservation-
ist, using those terms in their broadest meanings. To say that
the days of wild animals cooped up in barren cages and labeled with a minimum of common name and perhaps habitat
are entirely over would be an overstatement, but the trend is
strongly toward more than mere animal keeping. Recreation
and relaxation certainly play a very large part in zoo going,
but a nationwide survey indicates that a very large number of
visitors go to zoos for education, and that this trend has come
about as a result of introducing children to zoos as part of
their school experience. And of course how the zoo is ori-
ented will determine whether visitors take away more than a
memory of a day's wandering in pleasant surroundings
among unfamiliar wild animals. People *can* be induced to
realize, more or less consciously, what the ravaged environ-
ment, pollution, pesticides, deforestation, and all the other

modern perils are doing to wildlife—and to themselves. They even can be made to see that something can be done about it, and what zoos are doing for the protection of wild animals, the breeding of rare animals, and the preservation of endangered species. Many zoos nowadays stamp or paste on their exhibit labels for endangered species a symbol officially adopted by the American Association of Zoological Parks and Aquariums, an antelope skull with the legend *Vanishing Animal* imprinted across it. Even if its conservation message goes no further than this, a zoo's repeated warning is bound to sink into the minds of its visitors.

But there are many more ways of inducing awareness that animals have their own niches in the natural world, their own specific ways of life and behavior. Even when confined in the most uninspired moat or behind bars, an animal may be interesting to watch, but something is added if it can be seen in an approximation of its natural living space, as, for example, in any of the African plains exhibits that are fairly common in zoos. And how much more interesting and unforgettable to see birds, for instance, exhibited in large and beautifully planted flight cages—perhaps with the visitors actually among them—or in habitat exhibits so realistically fabricated (of fiber glass and artificial foliage!) that one can hardly be sure whether the setting is real or not.

A zoo, as a sign in the Bronx Zoo once said, "doesn't just happen." Somebody has to make it happen the way it is. That is the job of the director and his assistants, the curators, the exhibition and graphics men, the architects, and, of course, the business office and the income-producing people who find the money for the zoo's expensive essentials. Curators have to be "animal men" with the well-being of their collections always uppermost in their minds, but increasingly they have to know and initiate informative exhibition techniques. This is just one of the new challenges to anyone thinking about a zoo career today.

Zoo men themselves are aware of the need for special training to prepare candidates for the career, and some have set up programs for zoological trainees. The students may have a Bachelor of Science degree, or may be pursuing a higher degree, or may merely have demonstrated special aptitude. They are put on the staff, on salary, for periods of one to several years as assistants to the curators of the departments in which their interest lies. They learn the management of a collection from the curatorial level and, naturally, at first do all the routine jobs: handling correspondence and telephone inquiries, keeping records, and writing labels. But they also get the invaluable experience of familiarizing themselves with everyday zoo problems by working closely with the curator. At the end of such an intensive course they are usually equipped to take over responsible positions in their own or some other zoo.

How does one get the opportunity to learn on the job? In two instances I know of in the Bronx Zoo, the zoo simply advertised its openings for trainees in the then-published "Newsletter" of the American Association of Zoological Parks and Aquariums. The jobs carried the titles of mammalogist and ornithologist, and two of the first applicants sounded especially likely; each had kept animals at home, each had a B.S. degree, each had spent summers as field assistant in natural history surveys. They were asked to come to New York for interviews, and the meetings revealed pleasant personalities, enthusiasm, and solid knowledge in their own fields. They were hired.

The personality aspect is perhaps more important than a mere mention of it in passing would indicate. Curators work

Above left: An African plains exhibit can only suggest the appearance of the real African veldt, but it does stimulate the imagination.

Below left: Modern zoo exhibition buildings are often bold and unconventional. This is the World of Darkness in the Bronx Zoo.

New keepers get a lesson from the head keeper on the best way to handle a bird.

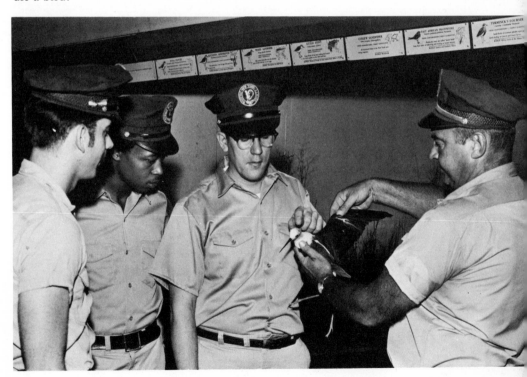

with people as well as with animals—the keepers in their own departments, their fellow curators, sometimes the trustees of their institutions, the general public. Tact, diplomacy, and stability have plenty of opportunities for expression.

Apart from the trainee programs of individual zoos, the future holds promise of specific academic training in zoo management. Currently (1971) the American Association of Zoological Parks and Aquariums has under consideration a syllabus for a two-year graduate program leading to a degree of Master of Science in zoo management, drawn up by Dr. Philip W. Ogilvie, Director of the Minnesota State Zoological Garden in St. Paul. The association hopes that some college or university will offer such a course to students already having a B.A. or B.S. degree. Possible candidates are referred to the American Association of Zoological Parks and Aquariums for information about the establishment of the course.

A zoo of course needs trained keepers as well as curators. As one zoo official puts it, "Keepers are our skilled workers. If we lost our plumbers, electricians, and carpenters, we could readily hire new people or contract their work out. In any case, the zoo would survive. But if we lost our keeper force, we could not function. And in an urban area we simply do not have a large work force reserve of persons equipped with zoo skills who could fill the void."

The difficulty of getting such people has led zoos in some major urban centers to give formal keeper-training courses through government-financed aid, with enrollees recruited from every walk of life. Probably an increasing number of zoos will offer such courses.

In this general introduction to the structure of a zoo, something should be said about zoo salaries. How good are they? True, it is unlikely that anyone chooses a zoo career simply because he thinks it is a good way to make money; other interests come first. A born zoo man is—a born zoo man. That is what he wants to be. Nevertheless, he is entitled to expect to be adequately if not abundantly paid for the privilege of doing something he likes, and this is generally the case.

Public zoos may be defined as nonprofit organizations (operated by a zoological society or by municipal, county, state, or federal governments), and salaries in the administrative and curatorial positions are not necessarily competitive with those in the profit-oriented commercial world. Still, at least in the larger zoos, they are likely to compare fairly with salaries in colleges, universities, and museums. Between zoos themselves, the salary spread in the higher echelons is considerable, depending on such factors as the wealth of the institution, its size, the responsibility placed on the executives, and so on.

By and large keepers and other nonadministrative personnel may expect wages in line with the going rate in the community for services of a comparable nature. Many zoos, as in other fields of employment, provide for periodical (often annual) salary and wage increases.

CHAPTER TWO

Getting a Foot
in the Door

I knew one zoo director who was in the advertising business before, as he said, he "got out of the rat race and began *exhibiting* rodents." His only qualifications were a liking for animals and a lot of administrative and public-relations ability. And good timing—he happened to be job hunting when one of the smaller zoos was looking for a director. He inherited an experienced, competent staff, and he had the intelligence to learn the practicalities of the operation before suggesting even small changes.

Any zoo man can think of similar stories. But a zoo director is a special case. Nowadays zoo directorships are likely to fall to the ambitious young men who are rising fast as the demand grows for imaginative exhibition; they have come up through the ranks with a solid background of animal management. Some have been curators of animal departments in their own or other zoos. A few have jumped from keeper jobs to a directorship. Generally speaking, those who were curators had academic training; and the keepers-become-directors, if their technical training was not so well grounded, at least had years of the most practical kind of animal experience.

The best way to approach a zoo career is through academic training in the biological sciences, though a B.S., M.S., or Ph.D. degree is no guarantee. A man may have a good academic record and even the added recommendation of field work in the natural sciences and still not be able to make the transition to zoo man. For technical training must be coupled with "animal sense," the ability to understand the ways and needs of wild animals in captivity, a vital concern for them, a genuine feeling for their health and proper exhibition. Animal sense is, in a way, inherent, and, in another way, something that can be acquired by osmosis, as it were, from experienced directors and curators—if one takes their precepts to heart and studies their actions and attitudes.

Now, what training does one need for zoo curatorship and whatever may lie beyond it?

Some years ago Dr. Frank N. Blanchard of the Department of Zoology of the University of Michigan, and Arthur M. Greenhall, drew up an outline of studies for prospective students of zoology. It suggested that while in high school students pursue studies that would meet the entrance requirements of the college or university they wished to enter—a program that the high-school authorities could help formulate. Blanchard and Greenhall used as an example the University of Michigan's entrance requirements for a freshman without conditions, and listed courses in zoology offered by the university as typical of those offered by other universities.

They strongly recommended studies of Latin, German, and French and pointed out that the latter two, particularly German, would be essential in the study of any science. Interestingly, they recommended taking "just enough science in high school to keep up your interest in the work." They also urged that students read the scientific and popular literature in the particular subject that interested them.

"Students who expect to specialize in zoology," they wrote, "should acquaint themselves during their undergraduate career with the fundamentals of botany, chemistry, physics, psychology, geology, geography, physiology, etc. They should also obtain a reading knowledge of French and German. A course in speech will also prove very useful."

The Blanchard and Greenhall advice to read the scientific and popular literature was probably the least needed in their outline, for anyone really keen on animals and zoos is likely to have been reading about them ever since he mastered the alphabet. Still, it is worthwhile expanding the advice by mentioning a few books and journals that might not be familiar to an aspiring zoologist unless he has access to a library with a good reference section; even so, only the exceptional public library would have, say, Loisel's *Histoire des Ménageries* or subscribe to "Copeia."

The technical literature on mammals, birds, and reptiles is enormous, and the flow of journals, handbooks, and monographs never slackens. Fortunately, most of the material need not concern the student, at least until he gets into his subject in college, although it certainly would not hurt him to have a sight familiarity with the tools he will be using when he has the responsibility for gathering and keeping an animal collection.

College and university libraries, and those of at least the larger zoos, are likely to have the important species catalogs and monographs, the big guns of the zoologist's armament; they belong in institutional libraries rather than in home collections. For one thing, they are quite expensive. True, monographs are often highly readable—Beebe's great "Monograph of the Pheasants," for example—but nobody sits down to read through the twenty-seven volumes of the British Museum's *Catalogue of Birds*. Nevertheless, when you need to refer to the work, it's helpful to know how to use it.

Coming down to the more practical level of the popular and semitechnical literature and the journals of the specialized societies, it is a good idea to have your own basic library, for the more you read about zoos and your own field, the better equipped you are. You ought to be able to pluck a reference book off your own shelves instead of having to go to the library—and likely finding that the book is unavailable. On the other hand, a generously equipped public library enables you to sort out the really informative popular books and the best general reference works without putting out a lot of money and perhaps finding that the books aren't what you want.

As a starter toward a personal zoo library, "Zoological Park Fundamentals" is strongly recommended. This eighty-page booklet about zoos and animal keeping was written by Lawrence Curtis, now Director of the Oklahoma City Zoo, and was published in 1968 by the American Association of Zoological Parks and Aquariums. It is inexpensive and may be ordered from the National Recreation and Park Association, 1700 Pennsylvania Avenue, N.W., Washington, D.C. 20006. Because this is such a valuable introduction to the zoo world, its section headings are listed:

Zoo Philosophy; How to Start a Zoo; Zoo Planning; Design Features (Grounds, Animal Exhibits, Service Structures, General); Operation (Administration, Maintenance, Animal Factors); Annotated Bibliography; Appendices (Data Analysis of Selected Zoos, Sample Tables of Organization for

Zoos, Sample Job Descriptions for Zoo Personnel, Sample Zoo Operational Budget Form, Sample Zoo Record Forms).

The booklet is well illustrated with photographs of ground layouts, exhibits, and graphic themes chosen from zoos all over the country. It should certainly be in the hands of everyone thinking of a zoo career.

A valuable predecessor, "A Zoological Park: Why, Where, How," first published in 1954 (now out of print), was drawn up by members of the Zoological Park Workshop at the Agricultural Experiment Station and Cooperative Extension Service of the University of Michigan at East Lansing.

Most zoo directors and many curators are active members of the American Association of Zoological Parks and Aquariums. There is also an associate membership (anyone interested in the profession may belong) that includes a subscription to a publication which gives news of recent acquisitions, important events in the country's zoos, staff changes, conservation trends, and, of special interest to zoo careerists, notices of positions available.

Only a handful of books and periodicals will be mentioned here, some of which are listed in the annotated bibliography of "Zoological Park Fundamentals."

The student is likely to have already the handbooks of his specialty, such as Roger Conant's *A Field Guide to Reptiles and Amphibians of the United States East of the 100th Meridian* or Burt and Grossenheider's *A Field Guide to the Mammals,* both published by Houghton Mifflin Company, Boston 02107; or Richard H. Pough's Audubon bird guides, published by Doubleday and Company, Inc., Garden City, New York 11530. Victor Cahalane's *Mammals of North America,* published by The Macmillan Company, New York 10022, is well worth having.

James Fisher's *Zoos of the World: The Story of Animals in Captivity* is good reading for the story of captivity, both historically and in the present day; it was published by Natural History Press, Garden City, New York 11530.

An old favorite of many a zoo man is *My Life in a Man-made Jungle,* by the beloved Belle J. Benchley, of the San Diego Zoo. Published in 1940 by Little, Brown and Company, Boston, it is unobtainable except through secondhand booksellers. Probably equally difficult to find is *Wild Animals In and Out of the Zoo,* by William M. Mann, of the National Zoological Park; it was published in 1920 as Volume 6 of the Smithsonian Scientific Series.

Anyone seriously interested in the history of zoos, and with a good reading knowledge of French, cannot do better than seek (and possibly even find through some bookseller specializing in natural history books) Gustave Loisel's *Histoire des Ménageries de l'Antiquité à Nos Jours,* published in Paris in 1912.

While they are expensive and may be beyond the means of many students, the annual issues of the *International Zoo Yearbook* are well worth having or at least consulting; many zoo libraries have the complete set. The yearbooks are published by the Zoological Society of London, run to well over 300 pages, and a typical volume contains sections on captivity experiences with a group of animals, new developments in the zoo world (architecture and construction), breeding, conservation, education, husbandry, research, statistics on zoos of the world, censuses of rare animals, and so on. Each subject is discussed in articles contributed by zoo people from all over the world. Special subjects treated in the volumes through 1970 are:

Volume I. 1959. Apes in Captivity.

Volume II. 1960. Elephants, Rhinoceroses and Hippopota-
muses in Capitivty.
Volume III. 1961. Small Mammals in Captivity.
Volume IV. 1962. Aquatic Exhibits in Zoos and Aquarias.
Volume V. 1965. Ungulates in Captivity.
Volume VI. 1966. Nutrition of Animals in Captivity.
Volume VII. 1967. Penguins in Captivity.
Volume VIII. 1968. Canids and Felids in Captivity.
Volume IX. 1969. Amphibians and Reptiles in Captivity.
Volume X. 1970. Birds of Prey in Captivity.

As far as mammals in the zoo are concerned, there is one
indispensable book, *The Management of Wild Mammals in
Captivity,* by Lee S. Crandall, for more than fifty years connected with the Bronx Zoo, first as Curator of Birds, then
General Curator, and at the end as General Curator Emeritus.
When it was published in 1964 by the University of Chicago
Press, professional zoo men referred to it as "the zoo man's
bible." In its third of a million words, it describes the characteristics of each order and family of mammals customarily
kept in zoos and goes into great detail about the care, feeding,
housing, reproduction, and longevity of animals in the Bronx
Zoo, with copious references to the captivity history and
practices of other zoos in the United States and abroad.

In the field of what might be called zoo animal husbandry,
there are three excellent books by Dr. Heini Hediger of the
Zurich Zoo in Switzerland. Written in German, they are now
available in English. *Wild Animals in Captivity: An Outline
of the Biology of Zoological Gardens* and *The Psychology
and Behavior of Animals in Zoos and Circuses* both are
paperback reprints of the English-language London editions,
published by Dover Publications, Inc., New York 10014. Dr.
Hediger's latest book is *Man and Animal in the Zoo,* published by Routledge and Kegan Paul Ltd., London.

A bewildering number of good books about mammals, birds, and reptiles in general (without particular reference to zoos) are available. It is impossible to do more than suggest a few that are outstanding because of comprehensiveness, wealth of illustration, or some other reason. Mammalogists will want Volumes 1 and 2 of *Mammals of the World,* by Ernest P. Walker, *et al,* published by the Johns Hopkins Press, Baltimore 21218. In ornithology, one of the most elaborate books is *Birds of the World,* by Oliver L. Austin, Jr., with illustrations by the outstanding bird artist, Arthur Singer; it was published by Golden Press, New York 10022. Students of birds will have many occasions to refer to the comprehensive *New Dictionary of Birds,* edited by Sir A. Landsborough Thomson, and published by McGraw-Hill Book Company, New York 10036.

Books in Doubleday and Company's World of Nature series are also recommended: *Living Birds of the World,* by E. Thomas Gilliard; *Living Reptiles of the World,* by Karl P. Schmidt and Robert F. Inger; and *Living Amphibians of the World,* by Doris M. Cochran. James A. Oliver's *Natural History of North American Amphibians and Reptiles,* published by Van Nostrand Reinhold Company, New York 10001, should be in one's library.

If the author of *Zoo Careers* may be forgiven for mentioning two of his own books, he would suggest *The Bronx Zoo Book of Wild Animals: A Guide to Mammals, Birds, Reptiles and Amphibians of the World,* published by Golden Press; and *The New York Aquarium Book of the Water World: A Guide to Representative Fishes, Aquatic Invertebrates, Reptiles, Birds, and Mammals,* published by the American Heritage Press, New York 10017. Both are obtainable from the Bronx Zoo.

Some of the journals and periodicals that students should

be familiar with, and perhaps subscribe to, are: "The Journal of Mammalogy," published by the American Society of Mammalogists, 1041 New Hampshire Street, Lawrence, Kansas 66044; "Copeia," the journal of the American Society of Ichthyologists and Herpetologists, Division of Reptiles, United States National Museum, Washington, D.C. 20560; "The Auk," published by the American Ornithologists Union, P.O. Box 23477, Anchorage, Kentucky 40223. Anyone who reads German will find much of zoo interest in "Der Zoologische Garten," published by Akademische Verlags Gesellschaft, Geest and Portig K.-G., Leipzig, Germany.

Now let us suppose that you have followed the prescribed courses in high school and college, have learned the realities of animal care by keeping animals at home and perhaps some of their natural history by field work, have read everything you could get your hands on, and, armed with your B.S. diploma, have managed to get a job in a zoo. You may have a title such as Curator Trainee, and you will definitely be rated as "junior staff." And how very junior you are will be made plain the first time you wave your diploma and charge into some animal situation you have only read about.

Here are some "Dos and Don'ts" for the guidance of beginners in a zoo career. They are quotations (sometimes expurgated) from the experienced director of one of the country's important zoos.

Forget your diploma. Learn from the people who have been doing it, not reading about it.

Get to know the people who are doing the jobs you will someday be supervising. Get to know the job routines.

After you learn the routines, then ask yourself how you can use the knowledge you've acquired in college.

If you think you already know it all, then you're in trouble. If you know you don't know, then you're smart.

Don't jump into a situation you don't know anything about, just to be doing something.

Hobnob with the keepers. You're going to have to depend on them to carry out your instructions—if you get to the point where you can give instructions. They may not have your education, but they have animal experience.

When you get to be director, remember you were just a kid out of school once, yourself. Don't be too hard on your junior staff.

It's all good advice.

CHAPTER THREE

Chief Worrier:
the Zoo Director

In those two words, "Chief Worrier," the late Dr. William T. Hornaday described his career for thirty years as Director of the New York Zoological Park. More than forty years later they are still the best short summary of the job.

"Zoological Park Fundamentals" devotes seven paragraphs to a sample job description for zoo director. They are pertinent, precise—and bloodless. Dr. Hornaday translated them into more personal terms. (I have omitted the quotation marks he was fond of using for emphasis.)

"Every czar of a zoo to whom ninety percent of freedom of action has been given (with only a request for results) thereby is made 100 percent responsible for everything that does,

---

Above left: A typical zoo director pose. There are always plans and problems to worry about.

Below left: Zoo men sometimes go on expeditions. Here the director of the Bronx Zoo (right) captures James's and Andean flamingos in the high Andes.

or does not, happen in his sphere of influence. The chief worrier of a zoo like ours in New York is responsible for everything therein that affects the public, the city government, the Zoological Society, 3500 helpless animals, the press, and the men and women of the force. His is a continuous performance of juggling with food, insufficient money, materials, new animals, old animals, deadly correspondence, and interviews—all to be kept going at once; and, believe me! thirty years of it should be sufficient to satisfy the most ravenous appetite for variety and work."

The zoo director is the chief worrier because his is the ultimate responsibility, however large and expert his staff. He coordinates, he plans, he looks ahead, he determines (with due reference to what his budget and the higher authorities— trustees or municipal officials— will permit) in which direction his zoo will go. He must dream and be practical enough to turn his dreams into realities. It is not an easy life.

Fortunately, very few zoo directors tumble into the job without years of preparation and toughening experience. They usually know animal management as well as their curators do, and they have the flexibility to direct and advise instead of ordering.

By the time one becomes director of a zoo, he is no longer exclusively concerned with the direct, daily management of animals. People and things and money are his daily and nightly concerns: resolving conflicts of personality, finding the money for all the demands made upon the budget, working with architects if the zoo is in a modernization or expansion phase, balancing priorities, making decisions. In short, running his zoo.

Some of the chapters that follow are narrative accounts of typical days in the working lives of zoo curators, a veterinarian, and an exhibition and graphics man in the Bronx Zoo. Details would vary if another zoo had been chosen for demonstration, but these chapters serve to show the kind of life an aspiring zoo man is getting into. By the time he works up to directorship, he will need no job description and no advice on how to do his job. He will know all about being a Chief Worrier.

CHAPTER FOUR

What Does a Mammal Curator Do All Day Long?

Not always what he thinks he's going to do.

For instance, I had arranged to spend a day with the assistant curator of mammals. He told me he generally started his day at eight o'clock by making the rounds of the mammal installations; he would pick me up at his office at that time.

I was there at eight o'clock. Jim showed up at twelve-thirty.

"Sorry," he said. "Houston Zoo phoned at midnight and asked us to look after a couple of young Indian rhinos they're getting from Basel Zoo. The plane was due at Kennedy Airport around six-thirty, but was two hours late. Then quarantine made us rake out the bedding and burn it. I had to haul the crates to the Animal Shelter and feed and water and change the straw, and then get them onto the flight to Houston. Let's try again tomorrow."

We did. There were no unexpected interruptions, and the day was what Jim called pretty routine. It could have been different in an endless number of ways and still be routine, for there is nothing static about a thousand mammals of sev-

40

eral hundred kinds. Little problems or big ones are met as they come along, and only one thing is certain: tomorrow will bring different problems, which will be handled with the same equipment of common sense, animal sense, expert advice, and experience.

Mammal buildings and ranges and corrals are spread in a dispersed but logical pattern over much of the Bronx Zoo's 252 acres. In earlier days the curator walked his rounds and still had time for the inescapable desk work—answering letters; writing exhibit labels; taking telephone calls from citizens with squirrels in their attics or raccoons at the garbage cans; ordering animals from dealers or collectors; reading the technical journals in his own field; posting the daily journal of births, deaths, and acquisitions; conferring with the head keepers or the veterinarian about shifting animals, or diets, or injuries; perhaps reading or criticizing a manuscript by a budding writer on natural history or advising an animal artist about the naturalness of a pose he had caught. The desk work is still there; it never goes away. But over the years, secretaries become expert in handling many of the telephone inquiries and take over much of the record keeping. The curator theoretically has more time for his prime business of supervising the management of his animals, but pressures have increased in the zoo business as in most other phases of modern life. The days are so full of physical motion and activity that—in the Bronx Zoo, at least—only by using the zoo's fleet of small electric carts can the mammal men cover their installations with reasonable regularity.

I had been recalling all these desk details and wondering how they were fitted into the program of a man whose day began at eight o'clock, when Jim picked me up outside the Administration building. His explanation was what I might have expected: he spends his daylight working hours doing the "outside" things that must be done; the paper work he does at home, at night or over the weekend. Sometimes, if he is lucky, he gets an hour or so at his desk in late afternoon— if the director doesn't call him in for a conference with the architects or on some other problems.

Zoos all over the country are changing, modernizing, building, and expanding as old concepts of animals behind bars give way to more natural habitat groupings and exhibits to show *how* animals live. Curators have to be almost as well versed in blueprints and specifications as in the art of animal management.

The impression I got from Jim and other zoo people is that clock watchers would not be happy in a zoo job.

Jim slid behind the wheel of one of the electric carts, built like a tiny truck. A Siberian husky was curled up in the back. He raised his head briefly and then settled down again. I knew him well: Dersu, reared from puppyhood by Brad, the curator of mammals (now on vacation). Accustomed to riding all over the zoo and making no move until ordered, as when a visitor sometimes found it amusing to "stir up the animals" by throwing rocks at them or climbing a fence to chase birds, Dersu was an effective deterrent to minor vandalism.

We rolled a few hundred feet to the Lion House where the keeper was perched on the guardrail, intent on a big outside compartment in which a heavy, wire-sided box was resting. The label read "Clouded Leopard," but no leopard was visible.

"He's stubborn," the keeper said as Jim drew alongside. "He comes out now and then but he won't go near the shift box."

The problem was an old and familiar one. The shift box —a portable crate with a door that could be dropped by the twitch of a rope—was a device for trapping an animal in its present quarters and moving it to others. The box was baited with meat, but the leopard was suspicious, and it might take a little time before greed overcame caution.

Shifting animals from one location to another is as routine as waiting for them to be trapped. Clouded leopards do not like New York winters, and this one had to be caught up and moved to indoor winter quarters. As Jim explained, it was early to make the change, but he needed the space; a male Siberian tiger had to be transferred into the leopard's compartment, in case the female tiger was pregnant. And the National Zoo in Washington was sending the Bronx Zoo a white tiger for publicity about tiger conservation, which meant that another compartment would have to be found for the puma . . . an unending game of musical chairs. (Incidentally the female Siberian tiger *was* pregnant, and a week later three cubs were born.)

The zoo's Alaska brown bear exhibit is a spectacular ledge of natural rock forming a high skyline against which the big brownies are sometimes silhouetted when they are not plunging into the deep pool at the foot of the cliff or sharpening their claws on fallen trees. When we arrived, Mickey, the keeper, was thawing a chunk of frozen mackerel in the keeper's room at one end.

Jim had news for him: seven new foxes were to be added to the bear exhibit. All were captivity-reared, five of them in the Winnipeg Zoo, where they had been accustomed to living with bears; they ought to adjust readily to their Bronx Zoo home.

Mickey is an experienced keeper, and he thought immedi-

Small electric carts make it easy for the zoo staff to visit widespread installations with reasonable regularity.

Above right: The birth of these tiger cubs in the Bronx Zoo set off a series of shifts of animals from one compartment to another in order to give the family privacy.

Below right: Brown bears are exhibited on a rocky ledge in the Bronx Zoo. Seven foxes were eventually exhibited with them.

In any zoo there is usually a baby animal that needs special care.

Even the curator of mammals may be drafted as an assistant mother to a zoo baby.

ately about the foxes' reactions. He suggested screening off the outside end of one of the tunnels leading from the sleeping quarters and letting the foxes get a look at their new world for a few days before turning them out.

Jim agreed they should be kept in until they got to know where their food was routinely placed and they could feel they had a place of their own. After they had learned about their own quarters, the keeper could lock the bears in and let the foxes run outside for a few days by themselves to get used to the whole exhibit.

The management of wild animals is the art of attention to small details. Mickey brought up one: the concrete paving at the foot of the rock ledge would have to be patched before the foxes were turned out. The floor was partly natural rock, partly concrete, and the bears already had ripped up whole slabs. The foxes would start digging, of course.

Jim made a note to ask the Construction Department to check the paving. His final instruction to the keeper was to order a box of a new canned feline diet from the Animal Commissary; the veterinarian wanted to taper off on the dog chow the zoo had been using and try the new diet.

We rolled on to the World of Darkness building. Jim unlocked the basement door and we climbed a stairway to the exhibition level, where the public hall was dimly lit and the exhibition compartments were bathed in eerie red or blue light that, to the eyes of nocturnal animals, is comparable to a starlit midnight to human beings. The building had been closed for two weeks while a new floor of rubberized material was laid. Soft and springy, like thick turf, it was not only easy on tired zoo-going feet but deadening to the shouts and exclamations of the thousands of visitors who streamed through the building on busy days.

All curatorial problems, it appeared, are not animal ones. A keeper unlocked three doors in succession, leading into passages behind the exhibition compartments, and tugged them open. The bottoms of the doors scraped on the new flooring—not much, a sixteenth or a thirty-second of an inch, but enough to tear the rubber. Another note went into Jim's notebook, another job for construction.

"How's the bat with the bad wing?" Jim asked.

"The wing healed, but it's lopsided. It still isn't flying well."

Through a door in the back we entered the flight cage of the fisherman bats, an open, thirty-foot-long exhibit with a row of small, black boxes on the walls at each end, and a long, narrow pool in the center of the floor. The bats, uttering ultrasonic squeaks, swoop back and forth over the pool when their boxes are opened and scoop up small fish from the water.

The keeper put on heavy leather gloves, opened one of the boxes, and picked a bat from the coarse wire netting where it was hanging upside down. He spread the left wing, and Jim examined it closely in the dim light. Some weeks before the bat had been found on the floor with one of its slender wing bones broken. The veterinarian had inserted an intermedullary pin in the broken bone, and it had knitted, but the alignment was not perfect and the bat wavered uncertainly in flight.

I wondered whether it would have to be destroyed, since it was having difficulty feeding itself, but Jim pointed out that the zoo has an obligation to its animals in sickness just as much as in health. He told the keeper to leave the bat with the others until the veterinarian could examine it again. He might be able to correct the condition by resetting the bone.

An African brush-tailed porcupine in the World of Darkness building

Above right: Its day and night life cycles reversed in the World of Darkness, a leopard prowls by day in a very realistic but artificial habitat exhibit.

Below right: Bats flit through this tropical exhibit in the World of Darkness. They are active in dim light by day and sleep when bright lights are turned on at night after the zoo closes.

Farther down the dark corridor we stopped to peer into a thickly planted jungle of tangled tree trunks and vines. The shadowy recesses were alive with silently flitting forms.

"We're breeding fruit-eating and nectar-feeding bats in there like crazy," Jim commented. "We don't actually know how many we have at the moment—can't count them in all that foliage. Anyway, the breeding proves the exhibit is successful; we're giving the bats conditions they like. The public likes the show, too, so everybody's happy."

The Bronx River flows through the zoo, and a new Bison Range was being created in a field beside it. The day before, construction had staked out a fence line leading into the shelter house, and Jim sighted down the line of stakes and made a note in his little black book. The angle of the fence made a tight place, a dangerous one because a bison bull could corner a cow in there and kill her. The staff had debated about that when drawing up the plans, and now the stakes made the hazard unmistakable—a "bug" that would have to be eliminated. Bugs are inevitable in most new animal installations, but the worst of them are usually caught before the animals are put in.

Jim spotted one potential bug the moment we struggled through ladders and lumber and wires on the floor of the Great Apes House, where workmen were finishing a complete remodeling job. This morning Mambo, a big male lowland gorilla, was to be introduced to a new glass-fronted compartment for the first time, and Howie, the keeper, was waiting for us in front of the barren exhibit.

"Those uprights," Jim said, pointing to two five-foot steel-and-concrete stanchions set in the concrete floor. "He could rip them out and pound the glass. I know it's Herculite glass, and it'll stop a gorilla—but not a battering ram."

The uprights were leftovers from the days when the compartment housed a family of comparatively puny white-handed gibbons.

Howie didn't think the uprights were a real problem. Mambo wouldn't pay any attention to them for the first few days, at least not until he got bored. The posts could be removed that afternoon, and in the meantime they were just something Mambo could scratch his back on.

Jim deferred to the keeper's proved expertness in gorilla psychology, and we waited for Mambo to emerge from the passageway from an inner holding cage. Minutes passed and finally Howie went behind the compartment to peer through a peephole into the inner cage. He came back to report that he had turned off the circuit breaker, which was feeding a mild electrical current onto the inner surface of the three Herculite glass panels that formed the front of the compartment. The device was the kind used to charge electric cattle fences, and its ticking—an unfamiliar sound—had made Mambo timid about venturing into the passageway. Ever since Mambo came to the zoo in 1951 as a sixteen-pound baby, he had lived behind stout steel bars. Now that he was being moved to a Herculite-fronted compartment, the mammal people thought the experience of a mild shock might teach him that a less visible barrier was still a barrier.

A few minutes later Mambo came bounding out and stopped in the middle of the compartment to look at us, the walls, the ceiling, the floor. His little brown eyes missed nothing and certainly not the heap of apples, bananas, carrots and shredded pineapple at his feet. After he had taken in everything, one enormous black hand shot out and scooped up an apple. Casually looking away as if he were not aware of us, he bit off and dropped pieces of apple until nothing was left but the core, then discarded it and selected a banana for equally careful peeling with his teeth.

"He'll do," Jim decided. "I'll have the posts taken out right away, and then you can let him in for an hour or so each day. Watch him all the time, though."

(Two days later Mambo investigated the glass and tapped it a few times. He must have gotten a shock, but he was used to the compartment by then, and the tingle didn't frighten him.)

Briggs, a big orangutan, was scheduled for the same kind of introduction to a similar Herculite-fronted compartment at the other end of the building. This time Howie suggested putting off the test until the metal strips on the floor, which established the ground for the electrified glass, could be embedded in epoxy. Briggs would start picking at the strips and never give up until he had ripped them out of the floor; that kind of persistence is second nature to an orang.

Jim agreed, and recalled an occasion years before when a rope was suspended from a toggle bolt in an orang compartment. The animal was always taking the toggle apart. Finally one of the zoo machinists swore he was not going to let an orang beat him, so he tightened the bolt with the heaviest wrenches in the machine shop. The orang took a couple of days longer than usual to loosen it. In fact, he derived great pleasure from working on the bolt. Zoos, Jim thought, probably ought to provide simple puzzles like that for some of the animals, especially the primates; they seem to like having something interesting to do.

We made a short run down to the Antelope Range, where Jim had instructions for the keeper. The Jackson's hartebeests had been separated, adult males in one corral and females and a young male in another. Now it was time to take the young male out and segregate him so an adult male could be put in with the females—otherwise the adult would turn on the young fellow and perhaps kill him. The females would be bred in the fall, and presumably a nice crop of babies would be coming along next spring when the weather was good.

A relief keeper happened to be on duty, so Jim asked him to put the instructions in his daybook for action two days later when the regular keeper returned. The relief man was competent, but it is always better to have an animal shifted when the regular man is on duty. He knows his animals better, and would be more likely to notice if anything starts to go wrong.

After making a note about a sliding gate that refused to slide, Jim headed for the Gibbon Islands and the muntjac corrals, nearly half a mile away.

The Gibbon Islands, thickly planted with willows and connected by stout ropes, are two tiny islets in a shallow lake where pelicans swim all summer. The gibbons walk upright on the ropes, or swing hand over hand along them, and thus have the freedom of both islets. Gibbons cannot swim and would drown if they fell in the water. One of the ropes was missing, and Jim made a note to replace it. Or possibly he might ask the head keeper to set box traps for the gibbons and take them in for the winter.

There was another little problem in animal management at the muntjac corrals. A young male, almost old enough to breed, was running with the females and had to be removed to avoid the possibility of babies in the cold months, in case the females weren't already pregnant.

"It's a funny thing," Jim said. "Last December we put a breeding-age male in for three months with twelve females —eight of them young breeders—and we didn't get a

single baby. We took him out and later put in a male not related to these females. We ought to know soon whether he's a producer. This might be one of those behavior things. Maybe the first male needed battle stimulation or something like that—a kind of male rivalry. Or possibly he simply wasn't any good as a breeder, and we'll find that the male who is unrelated to the females is the answer. Anyway, we don't want this young male in there to complicate things."

The keeper was not in the muntjacs' shelter—probably he was down at the Kangaroo House relieving the regular man —so Jim opened a series of doors to make an escape route from the females' corral to another enclosure on the opposite side of the building. Then he strolled quietly among the quick-running little deer until he isolated the young male, who was easily distinguished in the herd by a red-and-yellow plastic ear tag. Driving it in the right direction, onto the porch of the shelter and through the open doors into the spare corral, took almost fifteen minutes, but, as Jim said, "Now that's done and I can forget about it."

He could, of course, have left instructions for the keeper to do the job, but Jim has old-fashioned ideas about keeping his own hand in with actual animal management. He pinned a note inside the shelter, telling the keeper what he had done, and we left.

On the way to the Animal Hospital to pick up a small jar of ointment for a fisherman bat that had a chafed spot on one

---

Above left: Fortunately for the zoo curators and the veterinarian, elephants seldom create problems, and whatever they do is interesting.

Below left: A hippopotamus will expend enormous energy for even as small an amount of food as a single carrot.

of its wings, he drove through the service yard where the zoo's carpentry, ironwork, plumbing, and electrical shops are concentrated. Here he noticed a transversely sawed section of concrete sewer pipe lying outside a shop. Out came the notebook again. The pipe, tilted just a little, would serve as a good prefabricated feeding trough for the new Bison Range; one section of pipe split in half would make two troughs and save a lot of work.

The afternoon was wearing on after a lengthy lunchtime hiatus, prolonged by an Australian naturalist who was visiting the zoo that day. As we rounded the Monkey House, Jim noticed that the female Barbary ape was not back on exhibition; he had left instructions the day before that she was to be caught up from the isolation cage in the basement and returned to exhibition.

In the basement we found the keeper patiently waiting with his hand on a lever that would close the door after the ape had entered the capture box, where enticing food was spread out. She had gone in the box once, but backed out before he could close the door, the keeper said.

The ape glowered at us from the farthest corner and made no move toward the heavy wire box and the litter of fruit. She had been removed from the exhibition compartment upstairs so that three new youngsters could be introduced to the male without a family squabble. Now that things had settled down, it was safe to return her. The keeper could, of course, simply open the door a crack, reach over with a net, and snag her in no time. But she was a peaceful old girl, and Jim didn't want to upset her; it would be a great deal better if she walked into the box by herself.

Still, there was no point in wasting all day on such a job. Jim told the keeper to show her the net—put it through the partly opened door and wave it a little without touching her.

Most monkeys and apes have a strong dislike for capture nets—actually a net or canvas bag on a hoop at the end of a pole—and often can be moved in a desired direction merely by gesturing with the net. In this instance, the capture problem was settled within minutes; fleeing from the net, the ape scuttled into the capture box without being touched.

As we left the basement we saw a crowd gathered outside the Lion House, clustered mostly around the veterinarian's little green Animal Ambulance.

"The vet's giving feline enteritis shots," Jim said. "Let's go watch—it's quick and easy nowadays with a Cap-Shur pistol. Not like in the old days when you had to get the big cats into a squeeze cage."

But apparently injecting the shots was not going to be as quick and easy as Jim had thought. The two Siberian tigers due for injections from syringes fired at close range by a compressed, air-charged pistol were lounging lazily on top of an artificial rock ledge at the back of the compartment. The veterinarian had been unable to get away at feeding time, when they could be enticed close to the front, and now the tigers saw no reason to move. Their keeper called and wheedled, but the sleepy eyes merely blinked, and one of the cats yawned.

"I'll get them down for you," Jim said. "Here, Dersu!"

Spreading the crowd as the husky leaped from the back of the cart, he patted the guard rail, and Dersu rested his front paws on it. That brought instant action. The tigers seemed to flow down the ledge, then crouched and crept intently toward the dog. As soon as one flank was broadside to him, the veterinarian fired the first syringe. The pistol made a soft *plop* as the syringe entered the tawny hide and dropped off. By the time the keeper had retrieved it with a broom handle and the veterinarian had fitted another syringe into the pistol and injected the second cat, Dersu was back in the cart, and Jim was ready to call it a day.

A typical day.

Back at the Administration building he stuffed his briefcase with a pile of letters and journals to take home. It was going to be a zoo man's typical evening, too.

CHAPTER FIVE

Dull Day in the Bird Department

Joe, the associate curator of birds, warned me I wouldn't find much to write about.

"Go around with us if you want to," he said, "but we're doing just ordinary stuff right now. In a couple of weeks we'll be taking the pelicans in for the winter. The fellows go out in a rowboat and chase them ashore. Sometimes it takes nearly an hour, and maybe somebody will fall overboard— the head keeper did last year. Then you'd have something funny to write about. Or wait until December when we start putting birds in the new exhibits over at the World of Birds building. That's always interesting—seeing how they react to a strange home."

I explained that I didn't want to wait, and anyway I was interested in seeing what an ordinary day was like.

The day started with the most routine of curatorial chores —"running down" a new bird. In zoo language, running down does not mean physical pursuit; it is the search through the technical literature for the correct scientific name of a bird: genus, species, subspecies. Nowadays the tendency is

to disregard the subspecific designation and lump the races under a mere generic and specific name. The distinguishing characters of subspecies, or races, often are extremely minute, and if the books list many races, finding out exactly which one you have can be a frustrating job. Nevertheless, the Bronx Zoo policy is to run birds down to a subspecific name, if they have one. The day's problem for Joe and his assistant curator, Don, was to identify a new oriole that had been given to the zoo by a bird fancier.

Don had done some preliminary work and was certain of genus and species. The bird was known to come from southeast Asia, so Don looked it up in *Birds of South Vietnam* and *Bird Guide to Thailand*. Both books had colored plates and the new bird was illustrated, but unfortunately the races were not indicated—only genus and species: *Oriolus chinensis*.

To check on the possible races, Don pulled down one of the twelve volumes of Peters's *Check-list of Birds of the World* and thumbed the index. *Oriolus chinensis* had twenty-three races, distributed over much of Asia as well as many unfamiliar islands. Joe surmised, however, that the oriole would not be an island race, since bird collectors were unlikely to have been working there. More probably it would be a race with a wide distribution on the mainland.

Don ran his finger down the list and came upon two subspecies with very broad ranges through China and India: *diffusus* and *tenuirostris*. But which one was it?

Above left: The annual recapture of pelicans from a lake in the Bronx Zoo, to take them indoors for the winter, generally results in an unexpected bath for the keepers.

Below left: Clipping the toenails of a macaw is a routine zoo job.

Bird curator at work, weighing and measuring a young torrent duck

Metal identification bands, in all sizes and colors, used to clamp on birds' legs

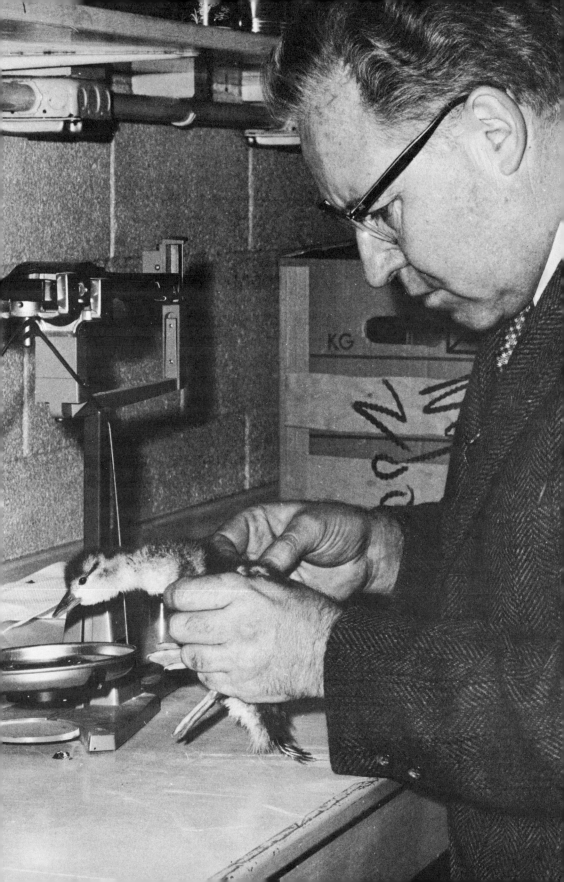

Joe was already reaching for one of the twenty-seven thick volumes of the British Museum *Catalogue of Birds.* It gave descriptions of both races, but the distinguishing characters were very close. He pulled down the four volumes of Dela- cour and Jabouille's *Les Oiseaux de l'Indochine Française,* and the French text yielded helpful details: measurements in millimeters of the culmen, or dorsal ridge of the bill, the tarsus, the wing, and the tail. Fortunately the difference be- tween the measurements for *diffusus* and *tenuirostris* was considerable. Joe jotted down the measurements, and it re- mained only to compare the new bird with them.

In a holding compartment behind the exhibition hall in the Bird House the bright yellow, brown, and black oriole looked down from its perch, unaware that its ancestry was in question. Joe entered the compartment and expertly snatched the bird from the wire. It pecked furiously at his fingers while Don applied a millimeter ruler to the diagnostic parts of its anatomy and compared them with the specifications in Dela- cour and Jabouille.

"It's *tenuirostris.* No doubt about it—*Oriolus chinensis tenuirostris.*"

"Good. Now all you have to do is write an exhibit label for it."

For the next fifteen minutes Joe and Don were deep in consultation with the head keeper of birds about suitable winter quarters for those birds that would have to be brought indoors with the onset of cold weather. This was an old story to all of them, for every fall hundreds of birds must be caught up from the summer-only aviaries, and the problem always is where to put them. To complicate things excruci- atingly, the zoo was preparing to open its enormous World of Birds building in the next few months. The new installation could swallow the entire existing Bird House collection without being half full. Hundreds of new birds were on order from collectors or dealers in Africa, Asia, South America, and Australia, and some were arriving every week.

The situation was critical because the main hall in the existing Bird House was temporarily unavailable as a holding reservoir. Two weeks ago the zoo had received a fine collection of touracos and barbets from a local fancier, and since there was room in the main hall, they had been put in those compartments. Then they began coming down with coccidiosis and roundworms and some other diseases. They were carrying the infections when they arrived, of course, but in their old home they were adjusted to whatever they were carrying and could live with it. Here they were under stress from having been caught up and transported and put in a new place, so their diseases flared up. The main hall had been closed and the birds isolated, but no new birds could be put in with them. Some compartments were empty, but could not be used now when they were most needed.

With Andy, the head keeper, trailing and taking notes, Joe walked down the row of exhibits and stopped to peer intently at one of the loveliest birds in the building, a blue-black-yellow-brown Gurney's pitta.

"How'd he lose those feathers between his eye and his bill? They were all right when he came in. Keep an eye on him."

The bare spot was too minute for me to detect, but both Don and Andy said they could see it. I chalked one up to curatorial carefulness and said as much.

"You train yourself to look for little things," Joe told me. "Anybody can see when a bird is in a bad way—slack, droopy, feathers not tight. Of course that pitta's in superb condition—did you notice how alert and interested he was?

Above left: The World of Birds building in the Bronx Zoo is setting new standards for bird exhibition.

Below left: The first bird is released in the Bronx Zoo's new World of Birds building.

A completely man-made, modern exhibit; the rockwork is a fiber glass shell. Several white-necked picathartes live here.

The little bare patch probably doesn't mean anything, but we'll keep watching him."

Later he pointed out another example of the "little things," the sort of information a bird man stores away in his mind. He had stopped at two adjacent exhibits, each containing a shimmering blue-and-black bird. One was labeled "Malayan Fairy Bluebird" and the other, "Burmese Fairy Bluebird." At first glance they looked identical.

"You get a new fairy bluebird with no indication of which one it is. It's simple if you already have an identified specimen—you just compare the new one with it and notice how far down the blue on the tail extends. It's noticeably farther on the Malayan's tail. That distinction is mentioned in the books, so even if you don't have another bird for comparison, the measurements will tell you.

"Or suppose somebody gives you a concave-casqued hornbill. I'll admit not many people have spare concave casques around the house, but one came to us just that way last week. There is no sexual dimorphism in the plumage of these birds —males and females are outwardly alike. You wonder whether the new one is a female that can live with your male. One look is enough: the male has a red eye, the female's eye is yellow."

Before we left the building, Joe instructed the head keeper to put three Andean caracaras in the central flight cage of the Vulture and Eagle Aviary that afternoon (the aviary had been empty for months while barriers of supposedly all-but-invisible vertical wires were being installed). As soon as they settled down, found their food pans and favorite perches, he was to move the female Andean condor out of the holding compartment in the Bird House basement and into the aviary with the caracaras.

Andy reported that the keeper in the Ostrich House had found a place for newly arrived Baillon's toucanets in the center section of the hall and had moved the perches to the top of the compartment; the birds were using them and settling down well. Joe was pleased by the Ostrich House man's initiative. He knew the toucanets were going to be exhibited in one of the treetop rooms in the World of Birds, so he had figured they were birds that naturally wanted to perch high. That is the kind of "bird sense" a curator likes to find in his keepers.

Joe had one final instruction for Andy: he was to tell the keeper in the Ostrich House to start using color supplement in the toucanets' food right away.

Wild-caught birds in brilliant natural plumage are inclined to fade in captivity. Scarlet ibises are a striking example; they may be an intense, glowing scarlet when they arrive, but pale pink a year later. Now zoos routinely add a concentrated carotenoid, a color supplement, to the diet of such birds, and their original color holds. There is much golden yellow in the plumage of the toucanets and a red streak on the bill; the carotenoid would hold both.

As we moved on to the Aquatic Birds House, Joe remarked regretfully on the loss the day before of a Cameroon finfoot, which had been found dead in the Jungle Stream exhibit. (The veterinarian had found a tumor in the bird.) Still, it had had a good, long life—twenty-one years. It and a finfoot in the Pittsburgh Zoo were the only ones ever brought into the country.

The basement of the Aquatic Birds House is a complex of storage bins for grain, of refrigerators for frozen meat and fish and white rats, a spotless kitchen, and holding cages for birds off exhibition. In a foot-deep concrete pool in a chilled

Above left: The swamp exhibit in the Bronx Zoo's Aquatic Birds House is realistic, with living plants, and sun bitterns regularly nest in it.

Below left: A dozen small birds live in this jungle stream exhibit. The massive rockwork is all artificial.

Boat-billed herons on a treetops exhibit, designed to show where the birds live

Sometimes birds can be induced to nest if at least the rudiments of a nest are constructed for them.

Keepers built a small nucleus nest for these hammerhead storks, using a woven African basket as a base. The birds went ahead and plastered it with mud and sticks, and laid several eggs.

room a drab young tufted puffin was swimming and swirling
under water. It had been hatched in the Sea Cliffs exhibit upstairs, but some of the adults started picking on the youngster,
and it was moved downstairs. Now the puffin was large
enough to be returned to the exhibit, but in order to get it
accustomed to larger birds, a couple of adults would be
brought down to share the pool for a few days. Afterward
the bird ought to get along all right.

We entered another corridor where twelve Inca terns,
solemn dove-gray birds with red bills and legs and down-
ward-curling white moustaches, were perched in two compartments, six in each. They had been trapped out of the
outdoors flight cage well in advance of cold weather. The year
before they had resisted being caught up, the cold came on
early, and a few got frozen toes and lost them.

"We're now breeding as many as we want, but did you
ever hear how we got our first one?" I had heard the story,
but Don hadn't. "Back in 1924," Joe said, "there was a radio
operator on a ship working along the west coast of South
America who liked birds and used to bring us quite a lot of
interesting specimens. One day when he was ashore he met
a couple of children carrying an Inca tern in a bamboo cage.
He tried to buy it, but they couldn't understand his poor
Spanish. He followed them home to a mud hut and tried
again when their mother came out to see what was going on.
He offered quite a sizeable sum, probably as much as the
family would earn in a month. But the woman shook her
head and came up with a phrase in English. 'Children's pet!'

"His freighter started north, and Inca terns were flying all
around, but of course there was no way of catching them.
That afternoon an oiler came up to the radio room and said
they had a bird in the engine room—it had flown down a

funnel and was flying back and forth in the propeller shaft tunnel. Since the radio man knew all about birds, would he please come down and take it away?

"So that's how we got our first Inca tern."

We strolled around the outside of the huge flight cage, noting which birds still had to be caught up and moved indoors. Several oyster catchers were milling around in a funnel trap. They were hardy enough to stay out all winter, but since they had trapped themselves, here was a good opportunity to trim their bills; zoo food was such that their bills did not wear down normally. Don made a note to perform the small operation tomorrow.

At the Ostrich House, the keeper was dicing apples and carrots and bananas and filling feeding pans. He had a problem—swimming pools. He had gone to a number of stores, but the swimming pool season was over and all the small plastic pools either had been sold or sent back to the warehouse.

I was mystified until Joe explained why the Ostrich House was in the market for swimming pools. Rockwork in the Penguin House needed winter repairs, and the penguins would be moved into the cool room in the basement of the Aquatic Birds House. That meant the torrent ducks, Inca terns, tree ducks, and so on, who normally use the pool in the cool room, would have to be sheltered somewhere else. The simplest plan was to set up plastic pools, the kind that dot suburban backyards in summertime, in the off-exhibition corridor of the Ostrich House.

Joe was not worried. The zoo's purchasing agent would keep trying, but if all else failed a couple of friends had promised to bring their pools down from the attic.

It was almost noon and Joe and Don went home for lunch;

both live in the zoo in apartments over one of the service buildings. When I returned to Joe's office at one o'clock, I found him going through a stack of letters and reports on his desk. His current worry, he said, was deciding what might be exhibited in the new World of Birds. The existing collection would supply many of the exhibits; for the rest, the zoo would have to depend on collectors in the field. Letters from collectors and dealers arrived in almost every mail.

I scanned one letter from Tanzania, which offered Egyptian vultures, a Gabar goshawk, pale chanting goshawks, dark chanting goshawks, and white-naped ravens. The zoo had no place for any of these, but Joe decided to write the collector and ask if he could send bee-eaters, wood hoopoes, barbets, trogons, woodpeckers, rollers, broadbills, and similar small birds.

Joe flipped through a little file of printed forms that recorded fecal analyses, sent up from the Animal Hospital. If a bird doesn't look right, the keeper takes droppings and sends them to the veterinarian, who reports his findings and prescribes treatment on one of the forms. More samples are sent later, and progress reports come back. A lot of paper work is involved, but it's a sure method of watching over a bird's health.

The rest of Joe's mail was "not very exciting." There was a request, referred to him by the director, from a professor at a technical institution to bring a class to the zoo for a tour of the Aquatic Birds House and a talk on the architectural problems encountered in designing a building to show how and where birds live. Joe phoned the head of the Exhibitions Department, who had created the artificial rockwork and had a hand in the elaborate exhibit decoration, to set a date next week when he could give an hour to the class. Another letter was from a conservation-minded candidate for United States

Senator. He wanted a meeting with the zoo staff to discuss restrictions that ought to be imposed by law on pet shops, forbidding the sale of birds, mammals, and reptiles either because their numbers were declining dangerously in the wild or they were so delicate that, in inexperienced hands, they were doomed to an early death. "Please work up the bird list and let's talk about it," the attached memorandum from the director said.

"That'll be a pleasure, and I only hope something comes of it," Joe commented. "Quetzals certainly are not pets, and they're getting scarce in the wild, but I've seen dozens of them in a pet shop cage."

He took "The Wilson Bulletin" out of its envelope and added it to a pile of journals, "The Auk," "Ibis," "Aviculture"—his night's homework. Joe reminded me that it was a dull day, a routine day, as he had warned me it would be.

I remarked that running down the oriole was interesting, and that I had expected more of that sort of work.

Sometimes there is more, I was told. But nine times out of ten, when a new bird comes in, one glance will reveal its identity; perhaps it's already familiar, or its habitat is known. The real fun starts when an immature bird arrives, and a detailed description can't be found, or the immatures of all races are practically identical. Then the bird is compared with the skins of immatures in the American Museum of Natural History, and—with luck—identified. At the worst, as has happened a few times over the years, there is nothing to do but wait until the bird comes into adult plumage. Joe felt that identification was an interesting but really a minor problem; most of his work was just housekeeping.

"Based, of course, on seeing the problem and knowing what to do about it," I commented. "And that takes experience and scientific background."

"Exactly. You have to understand the bird's physiology and its special life style—diet, courtship, nesting requirements, plumage changes. You need to know whether it's a gregarious form, what its climatic requirements are, and above all you have to be sensitive and responsive to its posture and the little things that tell you so much about its needs.

"Now"—Joe looked at his watch—"the radio this morning said rain and much colder tomorrow."

He dialed for a current weather report. The forecast was still the same, and Joe came to a decision about the afternoon's activities. He and Don had planned on digging out the brush turkey mound the next day, but it would certainly be more comfortable to do the job in sunshine instead of cold rain. I was invited to come along and take notes if anything interesting turned up.

I had already heard luncheon-table gossip about the five Australian brush turkey chicks that had hatched in the past three weeks from an enormous nest mound in one of the outdoor aviaries. The adult pair (the male is distinguishable by his wattle) are sizeable dark birds a little more than two feet long, and they are unmistakable anywhere because they carry the tail vertically instead of horizontally. In the spring the male had started scratching loose, sandy soil from the floor of the aviary and kicking it into a mound against the north wall. Knowing that the eggs eventually would be laid in the mound and that their incubation depended upon the heat of decaying vegetation, Joe and Don kept the aviary supplied with fresh grass clippings, which always disappeared promptly as the bird worked them into the rising heap of soil.

They never did know when the hen had laid her eggs. The brush turkey has not been studied in as much detail as the related mallee fowl of southern Australia, and some parts of

its behavior are not precisely known. Probably, however, the
hen and the male, or the male alone, digs into the mound at
night, working down from the top for about two feet, and
there the four-inch, white egg is deposited with its larger end
up. Over the course of weeks more eggs are laid at roughly
the same depth and, at least in the mallee fowl, in an irregular
circle. Some of the megapodes (or "big feet," as these incu-
bator birds are called) maintain a carefully controlled temperature in the mound as the vegetation decays. This is the
male's job, and he tests the interior of the mound daily by
thrusting his beak and temperature-sensing tongue into it. He
will not allow the hen to lay until the temperature is right
and the initial high heat is declining. He even regulates the
temperature by adding to the mound on cool, overcast days
and scratching off some of the covering on sunny, hot days.
When the eggs hatch, the chicks start digging upward and
emerge from the mound covered with dark brown down, but
with the wing feathers fully developed. They are ready to
begin feeding on insects and seeds, can run rapidly, and,
probably within a day, fly fairly well.

Of the zoo's five brush turkey chicks, one had died almost
immediately after emerging, one had been sickly but was
rapidly returning to normal under the veterinarian's care, and
three were thriving and growing. There had been no activity
at the mound for ten days, and the Bird Department was curi-
ous about what it was like inside—the disposition of the
plant material the zoo provided, what the eggshells revealed
about their distribution in the mound, the depth at which the
eggs had been deposited, and so on. Joe and Don collected a
shovel and a rake, and we drove down to the aviary.

With his tape measure, Joe determined that the mound was
three feet high, eight feet long and six feet wide. Though the
dark soil had a strong mixture of the sand forming much of

the aviary's floor, it was fairly cohesive, and Don had to push hard to thrust the handle of his shovel two feet toward the center. When the probes were deep in the mound, he got some readings with a thermocouple: 68 degrees Fahrenheit in one place, 74 degrees in another. A cool afternoon wind had sprung up, and the outside temperature was barely 50 degrees; the decaying grass was still doing its work.

Don started digging and as he threw the earth behind him and great chunks broke off and toppled into the hole, Joe raked it back and spread it over the floor of the aviary. In ten minutes Don had reached the center of the mound, and then suddenly there was a gleam of white and a gush of yellow liquid. The first egg had been encountered. It was fertile, too. In the crushed shell was a well-developed embryo.

Thereafter Don shoveled more cautiously and scratched the dirt away with a stick. Presently he uncovered a crumpled and brown-stained eggshell at about the same level as the first egg. From then on, for the next half hour, eggs and shells and one dried and partly disintegrated skeleton of a chick were uncovered; the chick had died while trying to reach the surface. Eventually the tally was sixteen eggs or remains of eggs. Interestingly, the whole eggs were snowy white despite being buried for weeks in soil that must have been soaked by the summer rains.

Don was digging near the back of the mound now and no eggs or shells had appeared for several minutes. Then a large chunk of earth fell loose and Don stepped back, then darted forward. He whirled around with a brush turkey chick in his hand.

"He was digging his way out!"

The chick, alive and vigorous, struggled strongly as Don passed it to Joe's cupped hands.

Scratching in the wall of dirt, Don pulled out a ruptured and still damp shell; the chick had hatched from it not long before. A few indications of the escape tunnel remained, and Don measured. The chick had scratched its way about twelve inches to one side and six inches upward, striking obliquely for the surface.

Joe peered intently at the little brown head protruding from his fingers, and then stretched one wing.

"Look at this!"

Most of the secondary wing feathers were open and functional, but the primaries were like gray quills, tightly encased in a fragile wrapping. The feather vanes were as snugly compressed as if they had been wrapped in cellophane except in spots where the wrapping had been rubbed off and the vanes stood out as in normal feathers. Joe gently touched the lower end of one of the wrappings and the gray material sloughed off and the vanes stood out.

Both Joe and Don had read everything in the zoo's library about brush turkeys but had found no references to casings around the wing feathers. They could only speculate that the wrappings might serve to protect the feathers while the chick was digging itself out, and that they had worn off by the time it reached the surface, or dried off soon afterward.

As it turned out, they had not read deeply enough on the subject, for feather sheaths *had* been reported many years ago by an Australian naturalist, A. J. Campbell, in his *Nests and Eggs of Australian Birds*. He merely mentioned them casually, as an observation of an unnamed friend. Still, apparently they had not been photographed, and Joe managed to get a good series of pictures before the casings fell off.

All in all, it was a most satisfactory ending to a "dull day" in the Bird Department.

Two Bronx Zoo bird men excavate a brush turkey's mound and take temperature readings deep inside it. The eggs are incubated by natural heat of decaying vegetation.

Above right: This brush turkey chick was clawing his way to the surface of the mound when the excavator's shovel uncovered him.

Below left: The outstretched brush turkey's wing shows the sheaths that cover the vanes of the primary wing feathers. The casings, casually reported many years ago, apparently never had been photographed.

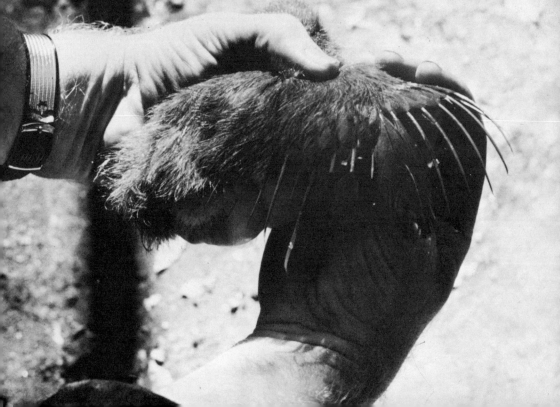

CHAPTER SIX

The Reptile Department Phone Never Stops Ringing

I had asked the curator of reptiles to tell me about his work—not so much the daily details as the broad outline of the job. During the half hour I was in his office he was on the telephone for about twenty-five minutes.

The longest calls were concerned with legislation for the protection of alligators and caimans, in which the zoo is deeply involved. Others were about sick turtles, a pet boa and an iguana that wouldn't eat; offers of turtles, frogs, and snakes from mothers disenchanted with the pets their children had brought home from summer camps; requests for information on setting up a terrarium in a school.

Answering the telephone, I decided, was the biggest part of a reptile curator's job.

Actually it isn't, for there are standard answers for many of the routine questions, and an experienced secretary can handle them. But if the secretary is out sick and the department's trainee herpetologist is somewhere between the office and the Reptile House, the telephone is almost a career in itself.

Primarily Wayne was concerned with the health and well-being of the collection, and then with the aesthetics of its exhibition. In the Bronx Zoo, ninety-five percent of the collection is in one building (only a few snakes, alligators, and frogs are kept in the World of Darkness building), and so the curator can concentrate his attention without all the running around that the Mammal and Bird Department men have to do. Wayne could make his daily rounds generally in less than an hour.

Overseeing the health of the animals is a basic responsibility of the curator, but having a staff of experienced keepers makes his job a lot easier. Wayne tries to go over the whole building the first thing each morning with the head keeper of reptiles; perhaps he may notice something that isn't quite right, or the keepers will mention anything unusual he has observed.

The zoo does not try to keep a big collection—about 250 species and subspecies and between 600 and 700 specimens. The object is not to show every kind of reptile and amphibian it might be possible to get. A natural history museum could do that better than a zoo possibly could. The Bronx Zoo prefers to stress their ecology and behavior, so the exhibits are designed to duplicate natural habitats as much as possible. Indeed, in many exhibits the visitor almost thinks he really is looking at a desert, or a tropical rain forest, or a mountain stream, or a quiet little pond, so the zoo tries to acquire reptiles and amphibians that fit into those environments.

Many exhibits and tanks are of course more generalized, and there is room for anything especially interesting that comes along. As an example, Wayne mentioned the banded sea snakes he had received recently. The zoo had not exhibited them lately and had no provision for sea water. It did have a suitable tank exhibit, however. These particular snakes have a salt-excreting gland in the head. In sea water they take in salt and continuously excrete it; in fresh water they would excrete their body salts, so rock salt is added to fresh water, which gives the gland something to work on. If the zoo wants babies to exhibit, the staff must put males and females together at the right season or note matings if the two sexes already are exhibited together. Later, there may be the problem of disposing of surplus young to other zoos, but usually someone is glad to have them.

Artificial vines and plants are so realistic nowadays that a zoo can do almost anything in the way of creating natural habitats. The Bronx Zoo was fortunate in having a large Department of Exhibition and Graphic Arts capable of designing exhibits that give the way-of-life story in a glance, working out the details from general ideas the curator might supply.

That, broadly, as Wayne explained it, is the curator's job: to acquire the animals, keep them in good health, exhibit them attractively, and tell the visitors about them through graphics and labels. As for the details of running the collection, the curator now had John, a trainee, to take over some of them.

The Reptile Department's young herpetologist illustrates one way of breaking into a zoo career. Reptiles had been John's special interest from childhood, and he had kept the common local snakes and turtles at home. After college he got a job teaching general biology in an upstate New York college, but he thought he would like to get closer to living reptiles so he applied for a job in the Reptile Department of the zoo. His background was good—experience in keeping reptiles and academic training—and a year later when the

curator found more and more of his time taken up with conservation of crocodilians, Galápagos tortoises, and Komodo
monitors, John's application was pulled out of the file and he
was offered a job as trainee-assistant.

It is certainly generally true that a good teacher makes a
good zoo man; both have the urge to inform. And there is
plenty of opportunity for information giving in modern zoos
as they break away from the old-fashioned concept of exhibiting animals in almost barren glass-fronted boxes.

Answering letters and taking telephone calls were the routine part of John's day. Now in the fall, people wanted to
know how to care for turtles during the winter. In the spring,
he coped with a different but equally standard set of inquiries, mostly about the venomous snakes that might be found in
areas where campers or picnickers were going. Identification
of shed snakeskins would come along later when vacationers
returned home with their trophies.

John had soon gotten to know the Reptile House collection and whether there was need—or room—for the snakes
and turtles that were constantly offered. Bog, spotted, wood,
and box turtles are protected in New York State, so when
somebody called in and offered one, John's advice was to
release it as close as possible to the place where it had been
picked up; otherwise the local fauna might be in a sadly
mixed-up condition.

Part of his job was writing exhibit labels. Any zoo man
knows a great deal of interesting information he would like
to put on a label. The Reptile Department used to write fifty
to sixty words of text (besides the common and scientific
names and the family name and habitat), but observation of
visitors' habits showed that labels of that length took too
long to read. Now John was cutting the text down to twenty

words or fewer, giving only the essentials that people will read and can remember.

It all sounded like pretty routine activity, and so it is. But routine is the largest part of a well-run department, and very little time is spent meeting exciting emergencies. In fact, John could remember only one emergency in the past few months. A boy in the city was keeping puff adders, Gaboon vipers, rhinoceros vipers, and Russell's vipers at home—all venomous, and against the law. One of the puff adders bit him, and his father took him to a hospital. The boy had enough presence of mind to have his sister telephone the zoo and ask for antivenin serum. The zoo sent it to the hospital, the boy was injected, and everything turned out all right.

Early the next morning I made the rounds of the Reptile House with the curator, the herpetologist, and Pete, the head keeper. It was warm and humid in the halls, and quiet except for the splash of water as the keepers hosed down the glass windows of exhibits from the cautiously opened doors at the back. Each door bore a stenciled injunction: "Think before you open." There were no emergencies, no particular problems except at the riverbank exhibit, where the caulking had loosened and water was seeping out around the glass front. Wayne and John discussed the possibility of plugging the leak without draining the pool, noted a concealed overhead light that had burned out, an artificial vine that had become loose in the background of an exhibit. . . .

Above left: Because he is deeply involved in conservation work, the Bronx Zoo's curator of reptiles spends much of the day at his desk.

Below left: Keepers crating a Galápagos tortoise for shipment to Hawaii, where a breeding project has been set up

All was quiet, but nevertheless Wayne looked long and closely into each compartment. Obviously he knew exactly where to look to see the inhabitants, although many of the snakes and lizards were partly concealed under clumps of foliage or, in the desert scene, inside a horse's skull on the sandy floor. Not knowing where to look, I missed many of the reptiles until they were pointed out to me.

Later I remarked to the head keeper that they seemed to know where every animal was at a given moment.

There was no mystery about it, he explained. Reptiles are creatures of habit, like everybody, and they have their favorite resting places where the temperature and humidity are right for them—one indicator to the keepers that everything is all right. If the reptiles are not in their customary places, something is wrong. Maybe there is too much competition on the floor from other inhabitants of the compartment, so a snake moves out of his favorite spot. Or he may need more heat, and he moves up high into the branches, because heat rises.

Those are the little signs a keeper watches for, which tell something about the animal's condition. So do its feeding habits. On ·the back of each exhibit is a feeding card in a holder on the door, and the amount and kind of food and the date are entered after every feeding. If a snake, say, misses two· or three feedings, the keeper looks up its earlier record cards to see whether it goes off food at certain seasons. Maybe the occurrence is normal, but if it isn't the snake is lifted out and examined for snake mites or whatever else may show up superficially. Probably it will be taken to the sickroom upstairs where stool samples will be obtained and sent to the veterinarian. In any event, the snake is kept in isolation until the cause of the trouble is determined. Some snakes are in trouble if they miss only one or two feedings. All their routines are marked down on the records; the keepers don't guess at what is going on. They *know*.

Pete explained the Reptile Department's record system. Every exhibition specimen in the collection has a number on the record cards and an identification mark. Some are toe-clipped, others have tiny, inconspicuous metal tags attached; snakes have numbers tattooed on their belly scales. The curator's secretary keeps the master catalog, and a duplicate file is kept in the Reptile House itself.

I suggested that the record system involved an inordinate amount of bookkeeping, but Pete denied this. The Reptile House is arbitrarily divided into sections, and each of the five keepers enters the records for his own animals, so that no one man has too much paperwork. Filling out accession forms, noting the tattoo number, the tag, toe-clip marks, or some physical peculiarity that serves for identification becomes a simple routine. The keepers are trained, too, to enter notes about breeding, or any unusual behavior. First, of course, they have to know what normal behavior is.

"A lot of people think snakes and turtles and lizards and crocodilians are all exactly alike," Pete said. "They aren't— they're all individuals."

John added the comment that anyone who had kept reptiles at home would know this, although he might not realize how different each individual can be until he works with them in considerable numbers. A snake certainly isn't "just a snake." Some species, for instance, will tolerate a certain dosage of antibiotic; others will die of the same dosage. Unfortunately, there is not a great deal of literature on the care of captive reptiles as there is of mammals and birds. Recently the zoo's verterinarian had gone to a meeting of the American Veteri-

Above right: Maintaining different climates in a variety of reptile exhibits, from a desert to a humid tropical forest, requires elaborate engineering.

Below right: In the desert scene, as in other exhibits, reptiles have their favorite spots for sunning or resting.

Between pairs of doors in the corridor behind the exhibits in the Reptile House, the button that rings an alarm bell is prominent. A keeper is never more than five feet from a button that will summon help.

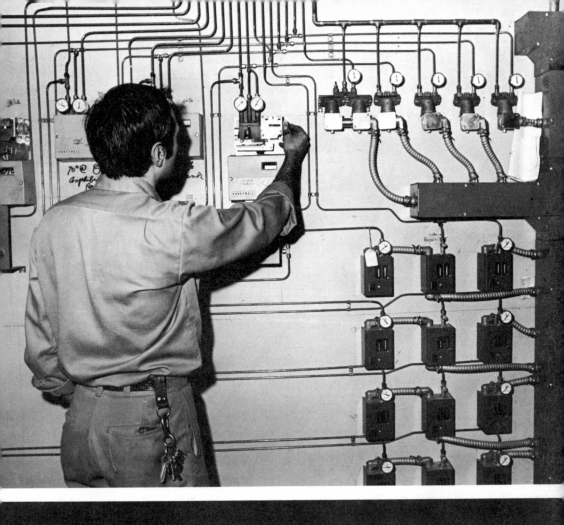

Above left: Record keeping takes a lot of the keepers' time. Here a reticulated python's egg is being weighed for the records.

Below left: Once a year this Cuban crocodile is caught up, for weighing and measuring.

The quarantine room in the Bronx Zoo's Reptile House

nary Medical Association and on his return reported that, while there were many papers on diseases of mammals and somewhat fewer on those of birds, not a single paper had been presented on diseases and treatment of reptiles.

Unlocking and closing doors as he went, Wayne toured the sickroom, the quarantine room, and the holding room (for reptiles not needed for exhibition) on the mezzanine floor above the exhibition halls. In the holding room hundreds of wriggling little tadpoles were swimming in shallow glass dishes.

I wondered how the department could keep record cards on every tadpole.

It can't, of course, as long as they are tadpoles; record keeping would start when they transformed and were large enough to toe-clip. They were the tadpoles of *Hyla vasta,* the Haitian giant tree frog. About two weeks before while the curator was making his morning rounds, he had noticed a sheet of little gray eggs in the pool at the foot of the mountain stream exhibit. A keeper's note on the record card said that the tree frogs had been seen in amplexus, the mating embrace during which eggs are shed into the water and fertilized. There must have been a couple of thousand of them, and half were immediately siphoned off and put into shallow dishes under different conditions of warmth, light, food, and oxygen, and in differing amounts of water. Nobody had ever reported hatching *Hyla vasta* in captivity, and the curator had no experience to guide him, except general knowledge of what tree frog eggs need. The eggs he left in the pool had died, but those in the dishes were doing well—tadpoles were hatching and thriving on algae and spinach and high-protein cereal for food. Wayne estimated that they would transform in a couple of months—and then he probably would have enough

Haitian giant tree frogs to supply half the zoos in the country.

There might even be another population explosion on the way, Wayne thought. The day before, South American poison frogs were seen in amplexus. They live in damp places, but they want water for their eggs, so the keepers created a little pool for them. More frogs to give away.

John admitted that he was still new enough in the zoo business to find a certain kind of excitement in recording the tree frog eggs and later reporting on them in the technical journal.

"It's a professional excitement," I said.

"I suppose so, though I had another kind of excitement the first week I was here. We were making the rounds one morning, and when we got to the quarantine room the curator made an X on my left hand with a marking pencil, handed me the feeding card for a new Indian cobra, and told me to lie down in front of the cage. Then he punched a button alongside, and bells began ringing all over the building. In about two seconds I could hear feet pounding on the stairs and doors being unlocked, and then came all the keepers in the building.

"One fellow whipped out his snakebite kit and began putting a tourniquet on my arm. Another chap grabbed the feeding card with its colored band and number and took off for the office downstairs. The tourniquet was on, and the first keeper was pretending to make an incision at the X by the time the second man got back with the box of cobra antivenin. Believe me, I was almost convinced I *had* been bitten!"

It was, of course, just a drill that the Reptile House runs through about once a month, unannounced. There has not been a case of snakebite in the building in six years, but the keepers must be trained to meet that emergency. They all

This cabinet contains packages of antivenin serum, numbered and color-coded to correspond with feeding cards on the doors to the exhibits.

The biggest snakes are not always the most dangerous. This Indian python has to be moved out of the way when its exhibit is being scrubbed.

carry snakebite kits with tourniquets and razor blades and suction cups, and when they are working behind the exhibits they are never more than five feet from an alarm button.

I had already noticed on the doors at the back of the exhibits that the feeding cards were white for nonvenomous and red for venomous snakes. All the venomous-snake cards have a colored plastic strip and a number that correspond to colors and numbers on the boxes of serum (kept in the cabinet downstairs) for each kind of snake. If someone is bitten, he is supposed to shut the door and snatch the feeding card that shows what bit him and what serum to use. Several species may be in a single compartment, but their bites require the same type of antivenin, so even if the man is in shock when help comes, he doesn't need to say anything.

"But the main thing," said the head keeper, "is to know what you're doing and not get bitten. Right?"

"Right!" said the curator.

CHAPTER SEVEN

The Veterinarian's Tuesday

Tuesday, the veterinarian thought, would probably be the best day for me to make the daily rounds with him. He would be taking blood samples, and a veterinary ophthalmologist was coming in to make eye examinations of any animal that had to be restrained. Since this was all quite routine, Emil felt that on such a day he'd have more time to talk to me about his work. Unless, of course, something unexpected came up.

Something did, of course. When I left the Animal Hospital late on Tuesday afternoon, the veterinarian had a 275-pound ostrich on the X-ray table and was fitting an anesthesia mask on its head. That had *not* been on the day's schedule; Emil had planned to spend the afternoon performing autopsies and catching up on paper work.

Still, before the ophthalmologist arrived and Emil began his rounds, we did have time for a brief talk about the job of a zoo veterinarian and how it differs from that of a veterinarian in private practice, with the usual run of cats and dogs, pet birds, and farm animals.

The training is the same; one does not "specialize" in zoo work. There are about twenty veterinary schools in the United States and Canada, and it takes two years of preveterinary study and then four more years to get a D.V.M. degree. No internship is required, and whether one goes into private practice, a government veterinary service, zoo work or whatever, depends on individual inclinations—and the opportunities. As for opportunities, every zoo no matter how small needs the services of a veterinarian. If it does not have a full-time staff doctor, it calls in a veterinarian in private practice in the community.

The main difference between zoo and private practice, it seemed to Emil, is that the zoo man spends a greater amount of his time on preventive medicine. He doesn't have to wait for clients to bring in a sick animal. Naturally, he handles sick cases as they come along, but he tries to prevent them from occurring. He is concerned with routine blood, urine, and fecal analyses, diet control, parasite control, and pathology. Inevitably he is involved in animal management and nutrition, breeding programs, behavior, transport, restraint —all sorts of things that do not ordinarily enter into private practice.

From his own prezoo experience, Emil recognized how interesting small animal practice can be. There is a lot of surgery, one can specialize, and a great deal of literature is available. The zoo veterinarian has a broader kind of practice, but unfortunately there isn't as much literature to help him and it is widely scattered. Actually, very little is known about the particular diseases of some species. When the veterinarian thinks he has something fairly well worked out, perhaps another species will pick up the disease, and it will appear in a different form, so the picture is varied.

If an animal gets sick in the wild, it generally becomes isolated and dies of the disease, or is killed by predators. In the wild there is seldom the transmission of disease, which is inevitable in a zoo with its more crowded and stressful conditions. However, by and large, captive wild animals are adaptable, and they respond to treatment.

As Emil saw it, with the exception of the restraint factor, veterinary *medicine* is about the same in zoo and domestic animal work. Treating a sick tiger is no different from treating a sick house cat, apart from restraint.

"The two kinds of practice each have their own excitement," he said. "Diagnosis and surgery, plus the challenge of the unknown in the zoo. For instance, we've been hoping to breed our takins. What's known about it? There is no literature. What is the takin's breeding behavior pattern? Did we go wrong in introducing a young male to an old female, and set up some frustrations? We just don't know—yet. Perhaps we should try hormones; they're successful in the musk ox and sheep."

By that time Roy, the ophthalmologist, was on hand and a keeper had brought in a mouse opossum whose stool sample the day before had showed a parasite infection. In the darkened surgery, Roy fitted his inspection apparatus on his head and peered into the animal's eyes, making low (and to me incomprehensible) comments as he did so. There was nothing wrong with the animal's eyes; Roy was merely interested in what he was seeing. Emil drew a sample of blood from a vein, and the opossum was liberated in a cage in the ward for treatment later.

The curator of mammals had reported that a male large Malayan mouse deer needed to have its thin, white, curved tusks cut back, and the simple operation was performed in

the kitchen of the Small Mammal House in a few seconds while the keeper held the little animal. Again Emil took occasion to draw a blood sample, and Roy examined the eyes and photographed them in depth.

The Ostrich House, where a variety of birds were in winter quarters, contained a couple of patients. An anhinga had a bad case of bumblefoot, and a white-fronted goose had been brought in from the shore of the wildfowl pond that morning, bleeding and unable to walk. Emil looked at the goose first. Half its body was bloodstained, and one leg was stretched at an unnatural angle. After a little gentle manipulation, the veterinarian repositioned it normally, bandaged it to hold it in place, and he and Roy went through their routine of drawing blood and looking at the eyes.

"You noticed that was the leg with the identification ring on it," Emil said. "The goose got the ring wedged between a couple of rocks on the rim around the pond, and when it struggled to get free, it dislocated the leg and ruptured a main blood vessel. The nerve is either cut or paralyzed—there's no feeling there, but it may come back. Let's give it a couple of days. If it goes gangrenous, we'll have to destroy the bird."

Bumblefoot is an unsightly and crippling but not fatal affliction that some birds acquire. When the keeper brought in the anhinga for treatment I remembered Old Nellie, a griffon vulture of nearly thirty years ago. She had such a bad case of bumblefoot that she used to sit with her feet thrust

The first suspicious encounter of two takins—a young male (left) meets a considerably older female. The Bronx Zoo hopes they will breed.

out in front of her—invariably in the front of the exhibit and facing the public—and it was difficult for her to perch or walk. The Bird Department finally took her off exhibition, pensioning her in a comfortable compartment in the reserve quarters because she was the oldest inhabitant of the zoo. She died a year later at the age of forty-one; the previous longevity record was some thirty-seven years for a griffon vulture in the Copenhagen Zoo.

The anhinga's trouble was by no means as crippling, but the puffy pads on the sole of one foot would get worse. Emil cut away some old necrotic tissue, sewed up the incision, and applied ointment. Then he bandaged the foot and returned the bird to the keeper with instructions to keep it out of water for a couple of days.

After examining a brush turkey with wing trouble and deciding to do nothing about it at the moment, the veterinarian went "eyeballing"—driving around the corrals and ranges to see whether any animals were in obvious trouble. Theoretically the keepers, head keepers, or curators would report anything that needed attention, but the veterinarian liked to make his own daily inspection. He went inside at the antelope shelter.

The patient there was an old female nyala. She had not been eating normally and was too unsightly for exhibition. She was also too old for breeding, and there was debate about destroying her. But Emil had worked on her teeth, she got back on her feet, and was now eating well. Her coat was still rough, but improving; she might come back and be returned to the herd.

At the Bison Range, Emil stopped to watch a bison cow and her calf calmly feeding.

"Animals like those," he said, "illustrate the difference between private large animal practice and zoo practice. If a domestic cow is sick, you just get her into a stall and treat her. Here we often have to knock an animal down with the tranquilizer gun first."

Beyond the Bison Range a herd of Thomson's gazelles were running with half a dozen South African ostriches, and I noticed a railing, about four feet high, around two feed troughs. The railings reminded me of the creeps for lambs on a farm, which indeed they were. The ostriches had been keeping the Tommies away from the feeding troughs, so the railings were put up. The Tommies can walk in and feed, but the ostriches won't bend their necks to creep under.

Just before noon the veterinarian went to the World of Darkness building to take cultures from walls and exhibits where there had been an outbreak of pneumonia. I arranged to meet him after lunch while he caught up with autopsy chores in the Animal Hospital's morgue, but when I got there the laboratory technician told me the program had been changed. The veterinarian would be in the hospital only long enough to pick up his equipment, and then he was going to the ostrich corral where one of the birds was having some trouble.

We arrived at the same time as six keepers from the Bird Department and walked warily through the big corral, keeping an eye on a pugnacious cock ostrich that wanted to join the party. The patient Emil had come to examine had been locked in a small corral in a corner of the range. It was upright, walking around, but there was a bloody discharge from the cloaca. A keeper had walked across the range at noon with feed for the gazelles and noticed a bloody stool on the ground. Nobody knew what was causing it.

Emil decided on an adequate dosage of a tranquilizing

Trimming the hooves of a zebra is one of the chores of the zoo veterinarian.

Above right: This forest buffalo is being maneuvered into a shipping crate after the veterinarian injected a tranquilizer (note the syringe in the animal's right shoulder). Tranquilizers make the job much easier.

Below right: Only after a tranquilizing injection can the veterinarian proceed to X-ray a gorilla.

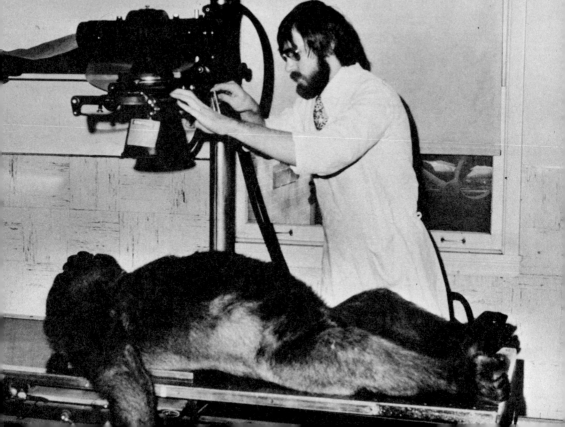

drug for an ostrich of that size, and in a few minutes had loaded a syringe and fired it into the bird's left thigh. The ostrich was not alarmed by the soft *plop* of the injection pistol and for five minutes continued to pace up and down along the fence. Then the slight trembling of the huge legs became more violent, and the bird stumbled several times. Finally it went down and the keepers were on it instantly, trying to hold it down as it struggled to arise. Its movements were so violent that one man was knocked over backward before ropes could be wrapped around the bird's feet and pulled tight.

The afternoon was gray and a biting north wind was swirling November leaves, but Emil shucked off his coat, rolled up his sleeves, and fitted a plastic examination glove on his right arm. Slowly and carefully he pushed his way into the cloaca but came up against a tightly closed sphincter that made it impossible to make an examination of the lower gut. After repeated attempts, he concluded that an X-ray examination in the hospital would be the only way of finding out what might be causing the bleeding.

The ostrich obviously was not knocked out sufficiently to make transport and X-ray safe, so Emil dispatched a man to the hospital to get a portable gas anesthesia machine and a truck with a lift gate.

The anesthesia mask was not well shaped to accommodate an ostrich's head but strips of cloth adjusted it, and presently the bird relaxed and its head rested quietly on the ground. Half carrying, half dragging, the keepers got it onto the tailgate of the truck and aboard.

Back at the Animal Hospital, it was simple enough to lift the ostrich onto a stretcher and hoist it onto the X-ray table. The veterinarian took three exposures and, since the bird was beginning to revive, administered more gas so it would be quiet while being moved to a hay-padded stall.

I could not wait for the development and examination of the X-ray plates, but I learned the next day that they revealed the trouble probably was enteritis, which could be treated as soon as cultures were examined. Emil was hoping that *that* day he would be able to perform his autopsies and catch up with his paper work.

CHAPTER EIGHT

Zoo Bedrock: the Keepers

Keepers are the bedrock foundation of a zoo staff. They are the men who are in there pitching with a manure fork and doing the rough-and-tumble work when any has to be done. They are closest to the animals—and the animals *are* the zoo.

There is no reliable, sure-fire test that will sort out good keepers in advance; their qualities, good or bad, come to the surface in the performance of their jobs. One thing they ought to have is animal sense, a faculty that is intangible but nevertheless real. One facet of it is the ability to see and understand a situation from the animal's point of view, and to try to figure out a problem before it gets out of hand.

Charlie is a typical "good" keeper in the Bronx Zoo; every zoo could match him and wish it had more like him. He was a farmer before he came to the zoo, and he watches his "stock" as if they were his own animals on the farm. Over the years he has been used in four or five mammal installations, big animals and small, and he was good with all of them. He told me once that when he was in the Kangaroo House he "equated"—his own word—the kangaroos to his sheep on the farm. He didn't think of kangaroos as something strange. He understood sheep, and kangaroos were kind of like sheep to him, so he had a feeling for kangaroos. When he was moved to the Antelope House, the antelopes became cattle. And in his present post in the Zebra House, the zebras were just horses.

If there's the slightest thing not just right with his animals, Charlie is on the phone to the head keeper right away. He doesn't walk away and leave the job at the end of the work week. Before his days off, or before he goes on vacation, he hunts up his replacement and tells him about anything he is watching—a pregnancy, or some animal that's getting rambunctious, or perhaps one that isn't feeding well. He has a sense of responsibility for his animals that all good zoo people have.

Many zoo men feel that a farm background is desirable in a keeper; a farm boy certainly knows all about hard work and usually a good deal about taking care of animals. The supply of farm boys is rather limited in the larger cities, however, and other qualifications are more likely to show up when applicants for keeper positions are interviewed. One good sign is that they kept animals as pets; another that they were interested enough to take biology courses in high school. Many keepers in the bird and reptile departments have kept birds or snakes at home, and are good amateur ornithologists and herpetologists. Or they may have gained experience by work in a pet shop, or on a game farm, or in an agricultural school.

The top keeper position in a zoo is commonly described as head keeper; in some zoos the job carries other titles but the position is the same. He may be in charge of the entire keeper force, or a major portion of it, or there may be a head keeper

Above left: Keepers spend a good deal of time making friends with their charges; mutual trust makes the management of the animals easier. This newly arrived young elephant had to be taught that it was safe to leave her stall and venture out of doors.

Below left: Food is a bond between the animal and its keeper. Here a young hippopotamus is learning what a nice fellow his keeper is.

This takin, from the mountains of Burma, came to the zoo when it was a baby. Now, as an adult, it has accepted the keeper as a natural part of its world.

for each of the animal departments. Many zoos have assistant head keepers who normally help the head keeper in his supervisory role and assume responsibility during his absence. A senior keeper most frequently works under the head keeper and manages an animal exhibition building through supervision of other keepers assigned to him and shares in their work himself. Lowest in the hierarchy is the ordinary keeper. He is the one who cleans, feeds, and generally supplies the close attention that a zoo's animal collection must have.

Not all zoos require minimum experience for appointment to the head keeper position, but the most common course in becoming head keeper is to proceed from ordinary keeper to senior keeper to assistant head keeper.

Zoos normally start new keepers out working alongside an experienced man; the right kind of beginner will learn fast and keep on learning. If he has the ambition for it, some day he may move into a top job.

CHAPTER NINE

Fishes in the Zoo

Nearly half a hundred zoos in the United States exhibit fishes as well as the usual mammals, birds, and reptiles. Most of these aquatic collections are comparatively small, with ten to forty species, but a few are so large that they take on the dimensions of a sizeable aquarium.

However large or small, the collections must be under the care of trained personnel, and there may be a curator of fishes, or an aquarist, in charge, and a staff of experienced tankmen. The tankmen (the job may carry other formal titles) of course correspond to the keepers in a zoo.

Management of more than a mere handful of fish species calls for training in aquatic biology, and students with an inclination for this specialization will need to seek out institutions that offer appropriate courses. At least a B.S. degree is certain to be required of anyone who wants to make a career with fishes.

The field is not overcrowded; trained personnel are hard to find. Indeed, the New York Aquarium, in 1970, instituted a program of curator trainees with the expectation that after

119

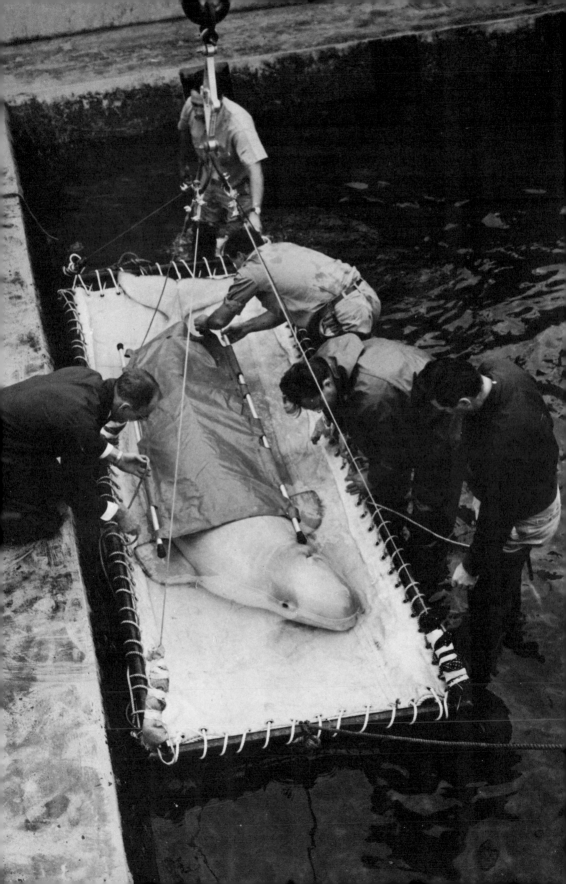

a year of experience under the supervision of its own staff, the men would be able to assume jobs in an aquarium, or in a zoo with important aquatic exhibits, or perhaps to specialize further in a fisheries research station. The trainees, incidentally, had B.S. degrees when they were accepted for training.

On the tankman level, a high-school education and practical experience usually are required. The experience may be gained through devotion to the tropical fish hobby (hobbyists do have to understand the basics of fish keeping), or it may be acquired by work with commercial tropical fish importers, or in some other field requiring skills applicable to the job. Naturally, a zoo with a fish section prefers experience or training, but as a last resort it may hire an untrained man and make a good tankman out of him, if he has a proved capacity for learning.

Two publications that should interest students looking for a career in ichthyology are:

Field Stations of the United States, "American Zoologist," Vol. 3, No. 3, August, 1963, published by the American Society of Zoologists, 333 North Michigan Avenue, Chicago 60601; and *World Directory of Hydrobiological and Fisheries Institutions,* published in 1963, by the American Institute of Biological Sciences, Washington, D.C. 20016.

The exhibition of fishes and aquatic mammals requires specialized techniques, such as this method of moving a beluga, or white whale, from one tank to another.

CHAPTER TEN

Exhibition and Graphic Arts

Exhibition and graphic arts specialists are the men and women who interpret the zoo to its visitors. The director of the Bronx Zoo put it forcefully in *International Zoo Yearbook*, No. 5:

"It is no longer sufficient to show a healthy animal in a cage physiologically adequate for it. It is, after all, not simply the amassing of a thousand species of animals which makes a zoological park of value, but the way the collection is interpreted to the zoo visitor. This interpretation is one of the most important distinctions between a good zoological park and a menagerie, a circus, or a freak show."

The quotation is from the announcement of a new Department of Exhibition in the Bronx Zoo, with a staff of four. Five years later it was called the Department of Exhibition and Graphic Arts, and the staff had increased to sixteen. Admittedly such a fourfold increase is unusual, but the zoo was going through a building boom and literally dozens of new exhibits had to be designed, built, and installed, and many of them incorporated elaborate graphics to supplement the

122

conventional labels. The alliance of contrived exhibit and graphics is familiar in museums, and adaptation of museum techniques to collections of living animals has often been attempted in some zoos in the United States and Europe. Significantly, more and more zoos are now hiring designers and exhibition specialists.

The exhibition people are the ones who look at a "physiologically adequate" but aesthetically unattractive cage and see it as it might become: a faithful replica of some typical habitat of the mammal, bird, reptile, or amphibian that has to live there. They have the skills, the new materials, and the tested techniques for creating a background against which the animals may be seen as they would appear in the wild— if indeed they could be seen at all. Who can observe the underground life of burrowing creatures except in such artificial but wonderfully realistic exhibits as the tunnel at the Arizona-Sonora Desert Museum, one of the pioneers in modern exhibition?

Graphics is a broad term that includes everything from the design and execution of large, pictorial, informative panels alongside indoor or outdoor exhibits to the artistic design of the zoo's printed matter. Graphics people are primarily artists, and they may work with printers, photographers, and silk-screen technicians.

They do not, of course, work in a vacuum. Their days are likely to be nibbled away by conferences and discussions with the director or the animal curators as they strive together to "get down on" designs that best bring out the points they want to make.

The problems and the kinds of work vary from zoo to zoo. Certainly in a warm-weather zoo, natural habitats can be more easily created by out-of-doors planting of live trees,

Signs, such as this, are typical of the work of a Department of Exhibition and Graphic Arts.

Above right: Part of the Exhibition and Graphic Arts staff in the Bronx Zoo

Below right: An artist paints a desert scene background for an exhibit.

shrubs, and vines than in northern zoos where many animals have to be kept indoors the year around or taken inside when cold weather comes.

The Bronx Zoo is in the latter group, where most tropical habitats must be simulated. While its graphics staff has about the same chores as graphics people in any zoo, the exhibitions side of the Department of Exhibition and Graphic Arts is currently under unusual pressure—a very large World of Birds building is nearing completion, the Great Apes House is being made over inside, and the formerly almost barren compartments for gorillas and orangutans have been transformed into artificial jungles.

I spent a few hours with Jerry, the curator of the department, and found the routine of his day very much like that of the curators of the animal departments, filled with conferences about designs, rounds of the workshops, supervision of installation of new exhibits ready to receive their animals. Similar activities are probably usual in every zoo that has an exhibition and graphics staff.

The first job of the day was to settle on the design of a graphics panel for the Great Apes House. The curator of mammals had indicated what points he wanted to make about the habits, habitat, behavior, and characteristics of gorillas, and had written a tentative text for the panel. The large display caption was to be "The Gentle Giant," and part of the display would dispel myths and legends about the ferocity of gorillas—myths born of the Tarzan stories and King Kong pictures. In Jerry's office the curator of mammals studied a colored sketch of the panel, prepared by one of the artists, and asked the graphics people to find a photograph of a gorilla laughing. They thought they could.

Text copy for the panel was obviously too long, and the

curator promised to return that afternoon with a shortened version, so it could be set in type in the Printshop and a silk-screen positive made. The gorilla graphic would start through the workshops the next day. Jerry was free of office work for the moment and ready to make his daily rounds.

In a shop across the service yard a diminutive woman in a paint-daubed coverall was outlining in white a life-sized figure of a man on a sheet of plexiglass. Similar etched drawings of a gorilla, orang, and chimpanzee were already finished and set in a frame so they could be edge-lighted, each in a different color. A flasher would illuminate the plexiglass sheets in sequence and show the comparative size and posture of the four primates. The last drawing, of the man, was almost finished and could be set in the frame that afternoon. Jerry moved on to the silk-screen studio and the Printshop to hurry along the shooting of plates for a new booklet, which the Printshop was turning out on its offset press. "The Children's Zoo Book of Recommended Pets" had a portrait of a guinea pig on its cover, and the printer produced an ink chart for Jerry to decide on the exact tone he wanted to achieve.

On trestles beside a huge copying camera that jutted into the room, I noticed the gibbon graphic, which the head keeper of mammals and his assistant had removed from the Gibbon Islands two weeks before. It had already been repainted where it was weather-damaged, and needed only another coat of varnish before being put away for reinstallation in the spring.

Hundreds of square feet of simulated rock were required for the new World of Birds building, and during the summer Jerry and his exhibits crew had made rubber molds of a 30-by-40-foot section of the vertical rock formation of the

Palisades on the New Jersey side of the Hudson River. There were thirty-one sections, and at the casting building three men were working with long-handled tongs to strip the rubber molds from the rock shells. A small mountain of "rock" was piled outside the building, numbered and waiting to be fitted into place. Some glittered with flecks of mica; they were unbelievably real, and yet a man could easily pick up the largest of them. Stripping was the last stage before the shells were moved into the new building to create a huge habitat exhibit.

At the World of Birds building, some smaller ledges were already in place in one exhibit, and workmen were drilling and tapping to anchor a shelf of "granite" on the wall just under the treetop-level window of a very deep compartment. John, one of Jerry's exhibitions men, was directing the work, and he pointed out a natural cup in a flanking rock. Eventually water would cascade down in front of the window and spray would certainly keep the flanking rock wet. "We could keep a live fern growing in there," he commented.

Two real—but dead—trees already had been set in place as perches for birds that live high above ground. Jerry noticed that a few small branches had been broken when the trees were moved, and he asked John to paint the ragged stumps to match the rest of the wood. Details were obviously as important in the creation of an exhibit as the small indicators that curators of the animal departments looked for.

Another huge compartment to be viewed from two levels was as yet barren, but the semicircular wall had been painted. Jerry and John looked at it from both levels.

"That room is forty feet high and almost as much in diameter," Jerry told me. "We want foliage green at the bottom, fading into a kind of indistinct green, and then hazy mountains in the distance. It's all right from the upper story, but from the lower level you lose the mountains. Better extend the foliage green up quite a way, John. The natural planting will cover most of the lower part anyway."

Jerry's last stop of the morning was at the Great Apes House to have a final look at a forest of fiber glass branches and huge, twisting lianas in the orangutan compartment before the glass window was set in place and the animals introduced to their new home.

The exhibit was beautiful; no doubt about that. If a section of the Bornean jungle had been transported bodily to the Bronx, it could not have been more real, right down to the texture and color of the wood and the encrustations of lichens. As a matter of fact, the exhibit was a faithful reproduction of an actual color photograph of a jungle scene. The only question was: would it stand up against the enormous strength of an adult orangutan?

The Mammal Department was convinced it would, for sound engineering principles had been built into that complex tangle. Jerry stepped over the open windowsill and shoved with all his strength against the liana nearest the window. It moved an inch or two, setting other great vines in slight motion, but the motion was allowed only by the heavy bolt eyes set in the ceiling; it seemed obvious that the network of branches was firmly fixed in place. Fiber glass is hard and inflexible, and no lianas were so small that an orang could twist or break them off. Besides, the vines were all tied together in at least three places, and to break one the animals would have to take the whole place apart. Even gigantic strength could hardly do that.

There was even provision for an orang's propensity for swinging and feeling the motion of a branch; one perch

Above left: Rubber molds being applied to a section of the Palisades along the Hudson River, from which lightweight "rocks" will be cast to reproduce the cliff in the Bronx Zoo's World of Birds.

Below left: Some of the castings made from the molds of the Palisades

In the orangutan exhibit, vines and trees had to be anchored to withstand the enormous strength and destructive power of the animal.

branch was devised to swing and rock, free of interference with other branches.

Jerry was ready to break off for an afternoon of sketching layouts for exhibits at the Zoological Society's membership meeting a few weeks away. As far as his department was concerned, the work in the Great Apes House was finished when the fiber glass trees and vines had been cast and installed. Eventually his sketches would be translated by his staff into a series of realistic exhibits that would tell, more quickly and convincingly than any label, something about the habitat and life of the animals that would occupy them.

That, in essence, is the function of exhibition and graphics people—to create natural settings for animals, to round out the picture of how and where they live. Flat, painted backgrounds may give some impression of habitat, but the three-dimensional effect that so many zoos now are striving for is incomparably more effective. That is why more and more zoos are engaging exhibitions and graphics people.

Graphics men and women get their training in art school; they are artists and zoo work is just one of hundreds of fields open to them. Art schools teach the special skills needed in zoo work—making casts of rocks and trees and vines, for example, although that is more the job of exhibitions than graphics.

A few of the Bronx Zoo's staff of exhibition men have not had special training, but under expert direction they have learned on the job. However, graphics people, who may be called upon for everything from designing and painting

Putting the finishing touches on a lightweight fiber glass tree that will be part of a habitat exhibit elaborate informative panels to drawing a cover design for a booklet, need art school training. Architects have a good background for that sort of work, and even a sculptor may come in handy. One of the Bronx Zoo's men is primarily a sculptor and is especially useful because he has a feeling for three dimensions.

My impression, however, was that exhibition and graphics people learn as they go along; no two exhibits are alike and all the solutions are unique. The jobs require training—and versatility.

CHAPTER ELEVEN

Publications
and Publicity

About forty zoos in the United States publish periodicals for members of the zoological societies that support them, for "friends of the zoo," for subscribers, or for promotional purposes. They range from mimeographed sheets stapled together to beautifully printed magazines of twenty to thirty-two pages, many with covers or inside illustrations in color. Some are frankly newsletters, announcing the arrival of animals, births, staff changes, expansion plans, and the like, confining their items to current events at the zoo. Many more periodicals have a broader outlook, and the acquisition of a new animal may be the springboard for a concise or even lengthy account of its natural history. Conservation and education are likely to be heavily stressed.

One issue of the Portland, Oregon, Zoological Society's magazine, "The Ankus," devoted five of its twenty pages to the threat of extinction facing the Columbian white-tailed deer. A whole issue of the San Diego Zoo's "Zoonooz" was given over to a "Sketchbook of East Africa," entirely in color. "Your Detroit Zoo" printed an entertaining account of the elephants that have been in the zoo's collection, and the zoological general curator prefaced his article with commentary on the threat to animals in the wild. The same issue contained an informative account of "New Zoo Diets." Cleveland's "Zoo News" gave the science teacher assigned to the zoo by the board of education two pages for a well-reasoned discussion of attitudes that may be formed toward the natural world through visits to the zoo. The New York Zoological Society's "Animal Kingdom" regularly publishes articles on the natural history of specific animals and on wild-life conservation. The society also publishes a technical journal, "Zoologica."

These zoo magazines, and many more that could be cited, are well-designed, well-printed, professionally polished publications. They reflect the concern of zoological societies for reaching out with natural history and conservation information, an extension of the zoo's basic educational function. It could perhaps be argued that all zoos, however small, would further the dignity of their purposes by issuing a periodical, even if it were only a four- or eight-page quarterly. Offset printing is relatively inexpensive, and copy composed on the typewriter reproduces well and saves the cost of typesetting.

Somebody has to write the articles, edit and proofread them, lay out the magazine, and gather the illustrations. The editor may work full time—often having other duties, such as public relations—or, on smaller periodicals, the editor may function part time and have some other job in the administration of the zoo. A background of newspaper or magazine experience, while not essential, is certainly a great help. In a noticeably large number of zoo periodicals, women are listed as the editors. The articles in most zoo magazines are "homegrown," that is, written by staff members.

Careers for writers-editors in zoos are by no means limited to periodicals, however. The amount of printed matter that issues from zoos varies widely, but it may include guidebooks, annual reports, educational leaflets, programs for special events, promotional brochures, zoo maps, appeals for funds, fact sheets for docents—and, of course, press releases.

A zoo's public relations man—if it has such a specialist—may also double as editor, or in the education department. Most zoos have excellent relations with their cities' newspapers and radio and television stations and can count on coverage when they have anything that will make a news or feature story. Indeed, getting publicity is seldom a problem for a zoo, so general is the belief in newspaper circles that pictures of animals and children can't miss. And when a zoo can offer an appealing shot of animal babies. . . .

Often newspapers and radio and television stations routinely telephone the zoo to ask what's new. Alternatively, the P.R. man, or perhaps the director, may phone in a tip and suggest coverage.

Publicity is of the greatest importance to zoos, for it brings visitors to see the newly acquired animal, the new animal babies, the new exhibit, the new building, whatever is freshly interesting at the zoo. The results of good publicity are likely to show up promptly in daily attendance records or reports of refreshment and souvenir sales.

Whatever the source of the publicity, whether from a staff public relations man or from a publicity-conscious director, someone has to carry through from the zoo's end and arrange the time and the place for an interview or for posing an animal for a picture.

Most zoo people on the level of director and curator are accustomed to community relations, in other words, making speeches about the zoo, the animals, collecting trips they have made, and the like. This activity could become increasingly important to the well-being of big-city zoos. The curator of publications and public relations of the Bronx Zoo has found it worthwhile to give a very large part of his time to community relations: serving on local committees, giving talks before service clubs and community assemblies, arranging supervised visits to the zoo. In general the aim is to try to create neighborhood identification with the purposes of the zoo and a favorable atmosphere among young people that may help cut down rowdyism and vandalism in the zoo.

CHAPTER TWELVE

Photography in the Zoo

In most zoos, there is someone around the premises who takes photographs.

The experience and equipment, however, of a zoo photographer varies. He may have no experience at all and only a Polaroid Land camera, or he may have been a professional for many years and work with the most elaborate still and motion-picture cameras the zoo can afford. About the only generalization one can make is that most zoos occasionally or routinely need to have their animals, personnel, and activities photographed. If they do not have a full-time staff photographer, at least they have encouraged someone on the staff in another capacity to take pictures on the side.

Over the years some of the larger zoos have accumulated very large photographic collections, often running into thousands of negatives. They may have been taken primarily for the zoo's own immediate purposes, but they are on file and accessible, and can be a nice if small source of revenue if made available to commercial users. Advertisers, publishers, artists, taxidermists, and students are routine customers.

The zoo's own uses depend upon the scope of its general activities. If it publishes a magazine, it wants its animals and scenes illustrated. It may want illustrations for souvenir postcards. Commercial postcard companies will do the photographic job if the zoo contracts with them for a given number of sets of cards, sending a photographer to the zoo for any length of time from a day to a week and producing a large number of color transparencies for selection. On the other hand, the zoo's own photographer, working throughout the year, will probably come up with some unique shots that an in-and-out photographer could not equal. The zoo's own man is right there when animals are doing something that may seldom or never be repeated.

Photographs may be wanted for publicity handouts, though most newspapers prefer to send their own man to cover a zoo story. But it may be a tight day on the newspaper's picture desk and no one is available when something exciting is happening in the zoo. On such occasions the zoo's own photographer has a good chance of getting his pictures used.

If the zoo has a graphics department, it is often going to want photographs of animals or part of their anatomy to illustrate panels describing their natural history or behavior. Pictures also are useful in the preparation of exhibit labels, and it is common practice to mount a photograph, preferably a color print, on a label. This is especially useful in bird labels for exhibits that may contain a large number of species.

The veterinarian may want photographs of pathological

A zoo photographer finds himself in many unusual positions. This one is photographing the locomotion of an African puff adder on a sheet of glass.

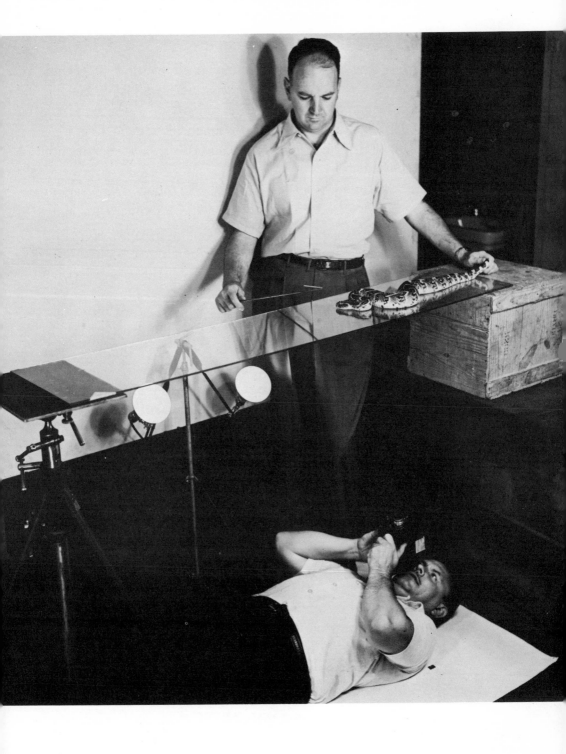

material. The business office may need pictures of scenes, such as a section of a walk or steps, where a visitor has had an accident and is now threatening to sue the zoo. If the zoo is in a period of physical change, it is good to have a record of the former installation and of the new construction in various stages.

Black-and-white negatives, either 35 mm., or preferably 2¼ x 2¼ or 2¼ x 3¼, probably will be standard for many years to come. Color transparencies are increasingly called for by publishers of books and magazines, however, and command a higher price than black-and-white, which is important to zoo income.

Very often the zoo photographer will be called on to take motion pictures as well as stills, so he should be capable of doing both. Probably many zoos do not have motion pictures of their own collections, because of the expense or lack of a camera and the man to use it. Yet the promotional uses to which a good 16 mm. movie, in color, with or without a sound track, can be put are almost unlimited. The most obvious one is for promotion in the zoo's own community. Films can be shown at schools, service clubs, church gatherings, and the like. Many things happen at a zoo that are fascinating when seen and enjoyed in the comfort of a meeting hall. And if the zoo is planning expansion, or raising money for some special purpose, there are few better ways of catching interest than by showing how engaging the animals can be.

Especially outstanding zoo motion pictures have some chance of appearing on network TV programs, and a still better chance on local stations. Some TV stations will take one-minute promotional films from the local zoo as a public service contribution.

Some zoos with a membership society behind them hold annual members' meetings, and a well-made film of the year's activities and new animals can strongly reinforce the members' ties with their zoo.

A photo librarian will be needed only when the zoo's collection of negatives becomes very large and the demands made upon it from its own people and from outside are heavy. Groups of animal prints can be classified zoologically and filed away in large envelopes, with the prints numbered to refer to the corresponding negatives stored in the standard film negative cabinets. The photographer himself, or perhaps someone else in the administrative department, can easily keep a sizeable photographic collection under control. The problem is that with today's minicameras and the prodigality of most photographers in shooting, a modest collection soon gets out of hand. The answer is the ruthless discarding of all but the best and most likely useable negatives.

CHAPTER THIRTEEN

The Education Department

A pertinent statement of the attitude of progressive zoos toward their educational functions is expressed in an article about a new educational building in the San Diego Zoo:

"The educational section contains classrooms, workrooms, and offices for staff teachers. It was felt there was little need for many classrooms since the zoo itself is used as one big classroom. Classes meet in the building with their teachers for an introductory talk and then proceed to the zoo for their lessons."

In a general way, every zoo is "one big classroom," but how much visitors learn in it depends on the effort the zoo makes to stress educational content. Informative labels, graphics illustrating habitat and behavior, Talking Story Books, guidebooks, information sheets, docents—a whole host of techniques can be used. Many zoos—and by no means all of them large—have buildings devoted to educational services. Other offices and departments may be combined in the structure, such as those of the director and curators, the library, publications, perhaps the photographic services. It

is a healthy sign that the need for classrooms and lecture
rooms, projection equipment, even student laboratories and
workrooms is now being recognized. Schools and zoos have
an obvious affinity for each other, and zoo directors are
aware that a strong working alliance with the school system
is a good thing to point to at budget-making time.

How much of a given zoo's informational program is
handled by its education department and how much is
divided among the graphics and publications people depends
on the organizational table and to some extent the budget.
Some zoos employ trained educators to head their education
department, or they may have college-trained graduates in
zoology on the staff. Many combinations of duties are possible. One person—a very busy one, admittedly—might or-
ganize school visits to the zoo, give lectures, conduct guided
tours, and even handle public relations and edit the zoo's
magazine in "spare time." Obviously, if the zoo's program is
fairly broad, more than one person is necessary to handle the
job. The one constant element in the zoo-education picture
is that more and more money, time, thought, and effort are
being put into educational programs.

The San Diego Zoo, among others, has gone far in education. Several years ago it organized zoo tours for blind, deaf,
and trainable mentally retarded children and later expanded
the program to include physically handicapped children and
those with speech problems. The work with mentally retarded children has been outstandingly successful, and one
of the teachers wrote, "Children who initially would cry at
the sight of a kitten have learned to venture into the animal
contact paddock alone and to stroke and feed the largest
animal there."

Many zoos have volunteer, unpaid docents who conduct

school classes and other groups on tours and give talks about the animals. Some have trained staff personnel to perform the same service and also take small, easily handled animals to school assemblies. The demand for such services usually is far greater than the zoo can meet. There may be formal lecture courses throughout the school year or in summer vacation months. In some cities the school board assigns a teacher to the zoo to meet with students and give them the kind of information that fits in with classroom work.

Because education, in the zoo context, is such a broad term and may spread over so many functions it is hard to be specific about the training necessary for a job in the education department. In one zoo the curator of education may need to know a great deal about putting educational motion pictures together; in another he may need to be skilled in writing pamphlets and educational leaflets; still another zoo may want someone who is able to function as a radio or television "personality" on occasion. In general, specialized training in the biological sciences—and versatility—are helpful.

Above left: The curator of education tells a visiting school class about elephants.

Below left: Introducing animals to children is an important part of a zoo's education department job.

CHAPTER FOURTEEN

Zoo Librarian

A professional librarian can be justified as a staff member only if the zoo has a considerable library—thousands of books (apart from those the curators may keep on their office shelves for constant reference) and hundreds of periodicals. Since very few zoos are in that group, zoo librarian is not a career one can confidently aim at.

Nevertheless, it may be helpful to give a short account of what a zoo librarian does. No matter how skimpy the collection of books and how few the periodicals that are routinely received on subscription or exchange, librarian functions must be handled by somebody on the staff.

As an example, the Bronx Zoo Library has some 14,000 books on its general zoological shelves (besides perhaps 1000 more that are kept by the curators of mammals, birds, reptiles, education, and publications in their own offices), and it subscribes to about 150 American and foreign periodicals and gets another 500 on exchange. The accumulation of periodicals has been going on since 1899, and despite occasional weeding out, when truckloads of minor or peripheral magazines are discarded, two large rooms are nearly filled with

bound and unbound magazine files. They are consulted sur-
prisingly often when somebody wants to look up an original
article to which reference has been made.

In earlier days the books were classified according to the
Dewey decimal system; in 1971 the librarian started on the
tedious task of converting to the Library of Congress system.

Books and periodicals are checked out and in, book and
magazine orders are placed, books accessioned, and binding
orders made out. The operation is indeed much like that of
any public library, except that borrowers and readers are
somewhat restricted.

Zoo libraries are often available to anyone taking courses
in the zoo, to docents, members of the zoological society that
operates the institution, and similarly qualified people.

A useful function of a zoo librarian is making Xerox prints
of the tables of contents of selected technical journals and
circulating them among all members of the scientific staff.
Anyone interested in a particular article can call for the
journal itself. An ideal supplement to this system would be
for the librarian to make brief summaries of articles most
likely to be of interest. "Biological Abstracts" does, of course,
do this, but the librarian's own abstracting service would
have the advantage of immediacy.

If the interested staff is small, and the number of incom-
ing periodicals not too large, it is a simple matter to spread
the new journals on an open shelf and let the staff browse in
spare minutes. Preferably a box of slips and a pencil should
be close at hand, so anybody who carries a magazine back
to his office can leave a note about it. However, this method
is not recommended if the zoo wants to maintain a complete
file of certain journals. In my experience, zoo people are like
everybody else in one respect: they are likely to carry a
magazine away and forget to return it.

CHAPTER FIFTEEN

Other Zoo Jobs

Zoology is not the only road to the zoo. Business and engineering lead there too. Somebody has to handle income and outgo of money, make up payrolls, buy supplies, manage food and souvenir services, supervise construction and maintenance crews, type letters, and keep records. None of these jobs require training in zoology or even a special interest in animals, and yet they might attract anyone who has prepared himself for some of the standard professions and skills in business or engineering—if it occurred to him that a zoo might need people like himself. He might find that work in a zoo offers satisfactions not readily found in other fields.

Not all of the services mentioned above may be under the direct control of a zoo. If it is operated by a municipality, they may be provided by the parks department or some other municipal authority. Comments made here are applicable mostly to zoos operated by an incorporated, nonprofit zoological society under an agreement whereby the society and the municipality share in operating costs and the services are largely under the society's control.

Some of the satisfactions of a zoo job have been mentioned

elsewhere, but they bear repeating. The surroundings, for one thing, are likely to be agreeable. Most zoos are adjuncts of large towns or cities, often located on the outskirts, and thus the staff may be able to live in the suburbs or the country, without having to catch the 8:17 and melt into the office-bound throng. Working hours are spent where the air is reasonably clean and free of pollution, where the loudest noise is likely to be the barking of sea lions or the whooping of gibbons, where the crowds are welcome because they have come to enjoy what the staff has to offer, and where the only routine is the lack of routine. There are trees and grass outside one's office, and the changing seasons to observe and enjoy. There is the satisfaction of working with people who are thrown together for motives higher than gain and profit.

I said earlier that training or special interest in zoology is not required for these jobs. But those who seek them should be warned: if they do go into zoo work, almost inevitably they *will* become interested in the animals all around them and may even find themselves giving learned lectures to their children when they take them to "daddy's zoo" on holidays!

So much for preamble.

Zoo Secretary. Good secretaries are always in demand; see the "Help Wanted" section of any newspaper. Often they are offered "glamor" jobs in a "prestigious" firm, with a chance to "met VIP's." Well, a zoo can hardly stand up against that kind of competition, but it is noticeable that zoo secretaries are likely to stay with their jobs a long time. They seem to like them. There is routine, of course, but even the largest zoo does not have a typing pool with all its dismal anonymity, or row upon row of clattering typewriters. Glamor is not a zoo specialty, although the offices are likely to be comfortable and well furnished (probably with African trophies) and the VIP's are eminent directors and curators from other zoos rather than movie stars. I do recall visits to the Bronx Zoo by Prince Rainier, Fidel Castro, and Emperor Haile Selassie (a lion cub nipped him on the ankle and made him jump), but unfortunately I don't recall that any secretaries got to meet them officially. The actual work of most zoo secretaries is about the same as that of secretaries in any office—taking dictation, writing letters, typing reports, keeping records, answering the phone. At least in the animal departments, however, their telephone conversations will not be limited to reporting that the boss is in conference; more likely a secretary will be telling someone the gestation period of an elephant (nineteen to twenty-one months), or refusing a garter snake or a canary or soothing some distracted soul whose parrot has just laid an egg "and it's the first time he ever did that!" (The answer to that problem is: "Don't worry. It's quite natural for a parrot to lay an egg. It won't hurt her." The secretary emphasizes the *her*, so as to pass on some tiny bit of natural history fact to the caller.)

The Purchasing Agent. Any purchasing agent must be accustomed to the feeling that he is standing chin-deep in a sea of paper—sometimes drowning in it—and the zoo purchasing agent is no exception. He is swamped by requisitions, purchase orders, bills, receipts, and forms. Professionally he is equipped to deal with them, of course. He has trained for the job in business college, and he probably has the fat volumes of the "Thomas Register" of all suppliers in the United States on the shelf beside his desk and scores if not hundreds of catalogs of manufactured products the various departments may need.

"My job," the Bronx Zoo's purchasing agent told me, "is

kind of like being the P.A. for a city. You have the same broad range of services and products to supply—hospital, library, offices, plumbing, electrical, woodwork, machine shops, automotive, sanitation, uniforms—even police badges. And animal foods. *And* the animals themselves. If the director decides to buy a pair of giraffes in the heart of Africa, the paper work goes through this office just the same as if a secretary were ordering a couple of typewriter ribbons. Of course, I don't have to locate the giraffes. I don't keep a file of animals for sale. But all this does make for variety in the work, and you're not always ordering the same old nuts and bolts. I like the job: might even stop and look at the new giraffes!"

Construction and Maintenance. These are two aspects of essentially the same thing: looking after the physical appearance of the zoo. They are vital services required by every zoo, since something always needs building and repairing.

The basic personnel, equipment, and materials are the same as in any construction and maintenance work: carpenters, painters, plumbers, electricians, machine shop, heavy and light automotive vehicles, wood, steel, glass, wire, concrete, asphalt, and so on. Only the use to which many of them are put is different—the housing and restraint of wild animals.

To give one example: a fence is a fence, whether it goes around a school playground or an airport, but it takes some tricky forms when used to confine a herd of wisents or a family of wolves. There is a whole science of zoo fencing and moating, and while the construction department may not be called upon to study it and know the latest practices— the director or the curators are more likely to keep up with such things—construction *is* called upon to build whatever is needed and to contribute its special knowledge of how the job can best be done.

The appeal of zoo work in construction and maintenance lies in its challenging variety and the fact that so much of it involves unpredictable animals and the need to be ingenious, to adapt materials and techniques to new problems. The supervisor of such departments must be able to do a little of everything: direct foresters and gardeners and all the mechanical trades, work with architects and builders, plan, schedule, meet emergencies, and—somehow—keep a dozen jobs going at once.

Revenue-producing Facilities. Most zoos have facilities or special attractions for which their visitors pay, apart from any entrance or parking fee. These can be enormously profitable and perhaps the major source of funds for the purchase of animals and for new construction. They are such things as restaurants, refreshment stands, souvenirs, children's zoo, children's farm, miniature railroad, sightseeing buses or tractor trains, aerial monorails, animal riding tracks, and a variety of other amusement devices. They may be let out to a concessionnaire, who returns a part of his income to the zoo or its operating authority, or may be managed by the zoo itself. In the latter case, the zoo needs experienced managers and supervisors.

Specific training for jobs of this kind is available; some

Above right: A zoo secretary works in an atmosphere of books and pictures and trophies, with the focus naturally on animals.

Below right: A zoo gardener has to be expert in creating natural exhibits with living plants.

colleges and trade schools give courses in hotel and restaurant management. There is also a new Revenue Sources Management School conducted by the Department of Recreation Resources Administration of North Carolina State University, in affiliation with the National Recreation and Park Association. The courses are not aimed at zoo operations—they are much broader—but they do have a bearing on zoo situations. An outline of the curriculum (obtainable from North Carolina State University, Division of Continuing Education, P.O. Box 5125, Raleigh, N.C. 27607) describes the school as "a two-year education program for park and recreation executives," and there are two annual one-week sessions of classroom study and lectures. The classes are held at Wilson Lodge, Oglebay Park, in Wheeling, West Virginia.

The Business Office. The complexity of a zoo's business office depends on the zoo's size, the sources of its funds, government research grants administered, whether investments have to be managed, and so on. There may be a comptroller and one or two assistants, or a whole roomful of people—an accountant, payroll clerks, specialists in one or another of the zoo's business operations. The training for comptroller or accountant is the usual one obtained in business college. Naturally most people who train for business careers go into private firms or public services, since there are not nearly so many outlets for their professions in nonprofit, zoological organizations. Still, where jobs do exist, they are likely to be broad enough to call upon all the skills one has learned in school and therefore be more interesting than the departmentalization of the ordinary business office. In a zoo, the comptroller probably will be the chief fiscal officer for the entire organization, and in the main he will be working with nonbusiness-oriented people. An unbusinesslike research man may have to be guided in the accounting for expenditure of his grant money, the terms of his grant may have to be minutely analyzed, and assistance given in the preparation of his application for funds. Contracts and matters of insurance will be handled, investments reviewed with the zoological society's treasurer, budgets prepared, costs projected into the future, analyses made of the zoo's revenue-producing facilities, endless reports prepared, perhaps new ways devised for exercising controls over income and outgo.

These are all normal business office functions, but the fact that so many of them are concentrated in the duties of one or two men is what makes the zoo business office interesting. As one zoo business manager put it, "Somehow, in the nonprofit zoo business, you have a feeling of real participation in something that matters, and a sense of accomplishment at the end of the year. Besides, you learn things; I always thought seals and sea lions were the same thing until I came here!"

Until he retired, William Bridges was for thirty-one years Curator of Publications for the New York Zoological Society, which operates the Bronx Zoo and the New York Aquarium. In that capacity he carried on a wide correspondence with young people who shared his enthusiasm for animals. Many were attracted to a career in a zoo, but did not know how to go about preparing themselves for such work. They wanted to find out what the opportunities were and what one typically does in the management of a wild-animal collection. Now this information, in expanded and updated form, is available in his book, *Zoo Careers*.

Mr. Bridges' own preparation for a zoo career is not recommended, for he flunked Zoology I in college. However, his dozen years as a newspaperman in Indiana, Paris, and New York were perhaps more necessary experience for the work of writing and editing the Zoological Society's publications, writing press releases, designing promotional material, and supervising the Photographic Department, the Printshop, and the Zoo Library. Zoological deficiencies can be made up when one eats lunch every day with such giants as Lee S. Crandall, Raymond L. Ditmars, and William Beebe.

Among Mr. Bridges' earlier books are *Zoo Doctor, Zoo Expeditions, The Bronx Zoo Book of Wild Animals,* and *The New York Aquarium Book of the Water World.* Since 1966, he has been Curator of Publications Emeritus of the New York Zoological Society.